LIBERTARIAN LEADERSHIP

UNITE FOR LIBERTY!

www.libertarianleadership.org

LIBERTARIAN LEADERSHIP

By
C. Michael Pickens

Gallantry Group Press
Sacramento, California
www.gallantrypress.com

LIBERTARIAN LEADERSHIP
Copyright © 2012 by C. Michael Pickens

PUBLISHED BY:

Gallantry Group Press
1900 Vallejo Way
Sacramento, California USA 95818-3845
www.gallantrypress.com
publisher@gallantrypress.com

Edited by Andrea Susan Glass and Theresa Wyne
Cover designed by Market Aces LLC

ISBN: 9780983963523

Printed in the United States of America
FIRST EDITION, 24 JULY 2012

This book is dedicated to my son, Mason,
and my two younger brothers, David and Brandon.
It's my purpose to give our future generations,
a better world than the world which I inherited.

ACKNOWLEDGEMENTS

Every thought, perception, and belief, every principle, idea, and ideal within this book was adapted from somewhere else or from someone else. They evolved from the hundreds of books I've read, the thousands of articles I've browsed through, or the numerous mentors I've learned from. The premise I live by is that there's no such thing as an original thought, no matter how original the thought may seem. It came from another thought, the seed of a thought that grew and matured over time, or from the combination of other thoughts.

I owe every bit of knowledge that I've gained to those who came before me. Those who've left their legacies within the pages of their lifeworks. My leaders. I'm deeply grateful to all of my teachers for walking the path and leaving the map for me, and for all of us, to follow.

Knowledge is one of the most valuable commodities one may possess. With that said, I would like to plant this idea in your mind, an idea that's grown into a majestic oak within my own mind. The premise is: "The more you know, the more you should realize that you don't know." This idea has grown within me and has given me an insatiable thirst for knowledge. But, don't be fooled by the fallacy that "knowledge is power."

Knowledge is not power. If knowledge was power, a set of encyclopedias would be the most powerful object on the planet. **Knowledge isn't power, but the correct use of knowledge is power.** It's the correct use of knowledge, the application of which we learn over time, that makes us wise.

We all start off life with the same amount of knowledge. It's the people who influence us throughout our lives who help to affect who we become. In the beginning, it's our family who influence us the most. I owe the most gratitude for my successes to my mother. She always believed in me and in my ability, no matter how crazy, unorthodox or off-the-wall of a direction I was headed, whether or not it was a direction she would have me go. Most importantly, she understood how stubborn and headstrong I was; she learned that to attempt to dissuade me would be a fruitless endeavor. She's always been a support structure and an inspiration.

At the age of 22, my first personal development course was given to me by my cousin, Amber Sturm. It was a rough time. I was drifting through life, directionless and uncertain. She gave me the gift that allowed me to identify my purpose. I haven't looked backwards since. I will always be thankful to her for the gift that has continued to give to me. It has allowed me to give so much of myself to others.

I would also like to thank the creator of that course, Jack Canfield, an invisible mentor whom I've never met, but hold in the highest regard. His courses have continued to guide me to where I am now and have been the rock that I've built my foundation upon.

Tom Liotta is like a brother to me. His advice, guidance, and occasional "reality checks" are most welcome. As far as the single most important influence and inspiration in my life, in regard to the principles of Freedom, Liberty, and the Libertarian Party, Dr. Ron Paul is my forerunner. My archetype. My leader. His 2007–2008 presidential campaign was my first exposure to the Libertarian philosophy. He opened my eyes as to what the nature of a peaceful and prospering society should look like; he's helped to direct me to the current journey I'm on. He is a true inspiration.

"Truth is treason in the empire of lies."
~ Dr. Ron Paul

CHAPTERS

INTRODUCTION

*"Those who expect to reap the benefits of freedom, must,
like men, undergo the fatigue of supporting it."*
~ Thomas Paine

Thomas Paine clearly understood that freedom starts at an individual level. The individual makes up the collective. It is our individual responsibility, our personal necessity, to educate ourselves on the principles of leadership in our own lives in order that we may affect improvement for the greater good of society. As more people take on this responsibility, the world, by default, improves.

This book is about arming you with the power to win the war for liberty, for the many battles ahead, for the hearts and minds of over 300 million people living in the United States. It is a veritable war, war of information, a war of knowledge, a war that's been raging since the beginning of civilization. It is a war that has no conceivable end. ***The war is, of course, that of Freedom and Liberty vs. Tyranny and Oppression.***

The biggest obstacle we must overcome to win this war is ourselves. Our limiting beliefs, our subconscious programming, and our self-created F.E.A.R. (Fantasized. Experiences. Appearing. Real.). Like the fear of public speaking, the fear of talking to strangers, and the fear of expressing ourselves, these things can't physically hurt us, yet most people are afraid of them. We often fear both success and failure.

Fear creates an inability to take action and to do the things we know we should be doing. We must constantly and consistently strive to build the emotional foundation within ourselves to overcome our self-defeating beliefs. We must rally others to our cause. We must motivate and inspire others to join with us and duplicate our efforts.

There's one thing we absolutely must remember, no matter

how many of our freedoms are taken from us. There's one freedom that can never be taken. It *is the freedom to choose one's attitude in any given situation.* We must remain positive and optimistic, as we constantly continue to move forward one step at a time.

To run away from the problem only creates distance from the solution. Admit that our fears are grounded in ignorance, yet know that we're not ignorant. Albert Einstein once said, "Condemnation without investigation is the height of ignorance." Whenever you feel afraid to do something, ask yourself where that fear comes from. Does it come from an actual physical threat or from the unknown? Is it linked to an action that is outside your comfort zone? Investigation is required in order to move out of our comfort zone. Forward progress is stymied by comfort. Fear is dispelled by knowledge.

The principles within these pages will help to propel the Libertarian movement to its greatest achievements. And that movement is the freedom that created the greatest country the world has ever seen.

"A rising tide lifts all boats."
~ President John F. Kennedy

CHAPTER 1

WHAT HAPPENED TO AMERICAN FREEDOM?

"The summer soldier and the sunshine patriot will, in this crisis, shrink from the service of their country."
~ Thomas Paine

During the beginning of the Revolutionary War, Thomas Paine wrote about the "summer soldier" and the "sunshine patriot." The "summer soldier" was a name for the Colonials who owned or worked on a farm. He would plant his crops in the spring, fight the British in the summer, and then go back home to harvest his crops in the fall. The "sunshine patriot" fought when things were looking good for the Revolution. When the weather started getting cold or there was an attitude of defeat, the sunshine patriot would sneak off in the middle of the night.

What have you done recently to help the cause of liberty? Is the extent of your patriotism to fly the flag on the 4th of July? Would you be called a modern day "summer soldier" or a "sunshine patriot," or are you nowhere near the fight that's currently raging for the soul of America?

As our freedoms have eroded, so has our country. America was built on the ability to do what other people around the world could only dream of doing. The American way of life was envied, desired, and loved worldwide. America was thriving, growing. America set the example and displayed the benefits of freedom and free enterprise. People from around the globe risked their lives to come to America. America represented a better quality of life.

The highest time of prosperity and happiness was when America blossomed at its pinnacle of liberty and freedoms. Americans were free to do business, taxes were low, and the free market could dictate which businesses would succeed or fail. The dream was alive and well, and everybody had the ability to engage. Many people owned their own businesses and added to the gross national product. Ideas thrived and continued to flourish in an unrestricted marketplace. It didn't matter if you were rich or poor, or what background you came from; in America, with a dream and action, you could become prosperous.

America was built by our free-spirited, hard-working, risk-taking ancestors. It was built on a dream of freedom from tyranny and oppression. The ability to dream and to take action created the greatest country in the world.

Do you have a dream? Would you like to live that dream? How would you like to create the lifestyle you choose for you and your family?

That's what America was. Not anymore. America used to be the freest country in the world when we flourished and thrived. ***However, according to the 2011 Index of Economic Freedom World Rankings, we now rank 9th in terms of economic freedom and 19th in terms of personal freedoms.***

The health of Americans is one of the worst in the economically developed world, and our country is declining rapidly. The sad thing is that most people have unknowingly been deceived about these facts.

We're no longer the freest country on the planet. America has more people in prison than any other country in the world per capita; we have 5% of the world's population and 23.4% of the world's prison and jail population.

To make matters even worse, our school system is ranked 14th out of the top 34 countries, according to the Organization for Economic Co-operation and Development, yet we spend the most money per child. Why is that? When our first schools were started, students were taught how to survive and thrive. Now, our children are being taught how to be good little followers and not how to think for themselves. You know there's a problem in this country when there's a hit show called "Are You Smarter than a Fifth Grader?" and most adults are not!

In our great nation's formative years, Americans were highly educated. Yes, American children achieved a higher education compared to children today. ***They were taught critical thinking skills, how to think for themselves, and how to solve complex problems.***

Children back then were taught how to step successfully into adulthood. In today's world, some children don't move out of the house until they're 25 or 30 years old, and many still don't know how to balance a checkbook. The subjects and skills they're taught in school don't fully prepare the students for the real world. Not even in college.

Our two-party system has had a horrendous effect on American lives. The international policy of conquer and occupy has generated an overwhelming hatred for America, and that puts our lives in danger. America currently has troops stationed in over 150 countries. How would you feel if China, Russia, or any other country pushed their way into America, set up troops, and forced their way of life and beliefs on you? Would you defend yourself?

Well, other countries are defending themselves at the cost of the lives of America's children. I find it odd that we only care about human rights and democracy in countries that possess large oil reserves, while in other countries where genocide is publicly rampant, we suddenly lose our interest in democracy and human rights. You do not commonly hear about those countries' problems in the two-party American media.

The safety of the American people has been greatly compromised. Based upon fear, the rights of Americans have been shattered by bills such as the Patriot Act, the National Defense Authorization Act, and the National Defense Resources Preparedness Executive Order. Every passing of such bills takes the U.S. closer to those ideals we despise.

America spends more money on our military than any other country in the world. Global, annual, military spending for 2010 was over $1.6 trillion, with the U.S. accounting for 43% of the total. In 1948 the Department of War was changed to the Department of Defense. The government's offensive ways of war are easier to swallow under the name Department of Defense. Yes, it's prudent to protect ourselves and our freedoms from an enemy, foreign or domestic, that attacks our land, liberties, or way of life. At that time America will stand tall and proud. America will fight with the heart of our forefathers. America will succeed in retaining our God-given, unalienable rights.

That time is now! It is time we stop the erosion of America from the inside. It is time to upgrade our international policy to what it was when we were loved, envied, and respected by the rest of the world. It is time to restore all the rights that have been taken from us through the legislative branch under the guise of protection.

We've been taught that we have the right to be happy. But, we really don't have that right! ***According to the constitution, we have the right to pursue happiness.*** It is our right to pursue happiness. However, we're limited in our pursuit of happiness because of regulative burdens.

The pursuit of happiness should be unabated by government policies based on one man's morality vs. another man's morality. We should be able to live our lives as we choose as long as we're not infringing upon the rights of anyone else.

Through politics as usual, we've seen a great decline in our country, in our economy, and in our liberty. We must get back to that which made us great.

Statistics show that 70% of new jobs come from small business. Yet, big business and powerful unions have bought up the politicians, and through unnecessary legislative regulation, the free marketplace has been bogged down, making it difficult for the little guy to work, to do business, and to succeed.

If you were to study the history of the fall of Rome or the fall of Egypt, you would find that America is escalating into the same error that brought about the demise of other powerful countries throughout history. Those countries' governments started taking more and more freedoms away from the people. Whenever you start taking away the citizens' ability to grow and to dream, your country will go into decline. It has no choice.

Healthy competition and the free market promote higher quality products and lower prices. Some people say we have a free market. But when you have to pay for licensing, permits, fines, and fees, plus additional unreasonable fines and unrealistic fees, it's no longer "free," and you may not even be able to afford to start a business. Too many laws are being created to stifle the minds and creative pursuits of the everyday person.

How would you like to have a free and open mind? Free to grow and create, to innovate and empower people to greatness? It's your God-given, unalienable right to pursue happiness. It's your right to fulfill your purpose.

Ask yourself this. Are the currently active politicians looking after your best interests, or are they only looking after themselves? Let's take a look at that. If they were looking after you, wouldn't you have the same retirement plans as they do? But you don't. Why? Because the current politicians abide by a completely different set of rules than the rest of us. They have adjudicated these advantageous rules for themselves. Approximately 58% of members of congress are millionaires. Coincidence? I think not.

When we were free, we had greatness. Now that our freedoms have been stripped, our country is careening into poverty. We're enslaving our children into debt.

I have a son. He's the reason I'm so passionate about this cause. We are here to rebuild a country, and to leave a legacy: a legacy of freedom, a legacy the next generation can be proud of, a legacy that gives all Americans a better life. We're passing the torch to the next generation, asking them to continue greatness. We should never leave the next generation worse off than we are. We should always be moving forward.

Many people have been taught for years that it's the norm to get a job, work for someone else, and do what they're told. They know nothing else. They have no desire or ability to start their own business and to think above and beyond what they have now or to reach for more. More for their friends, more for their family, more for themselves.

We must start teaching critical thinking. We're all made of the same material, which means we all have the same abilities. We're all born pure of heart and mind, but conditioned to be a certain way through our childhood, our upbringing, and our families, through our friends, our teachers, and the media. These influencers can only draw from the way they have interacted with the world based upon the way the world has interacted back with them. Children are programmed by their environments and take that programming into adulthood.

So, how do we overcome that conditioning? We overcome it by educating ourselves and others, with education that teaches how to think critically, to figure out solutions to complex problems, and to communicate in ways that promote continuous growth. Instead of tearing people down, it builds people up.

You're either growing or you're dying! You're either moving forward or you're moving backward. There's no standing still, because everything around us is constantly changing. Therefore, we have to be awake, we have to pay attention, and we have to get rid of the distractions in our lives that get us off track.

Now, what can we do to get our country back on

track? Not only what can we do, but what must we do? Now that we see the problems, we all have an obligation to do something, to find solutions, and to implement them!

> *Total U.S. federal debt has increased every year from 2000 to 2010, growing from $5.7 trillion as of September 2000 to $13.6 trillion by September 2010.*

If a person were to run their finances like the government does, they would be in jail. If they ran a corporation like the government does, it would be out of business. The government keeps taking from us until there's no more to take, and that's when we endure complete and utter collapse.

The two-party system is bloated beyond its capacity to be effective. It is time for a new birth. A new birth will happen when ideas and imagination, fueled by belief, inspire people to come together and put their hands to the plow. You won't be given what you need; you'll be given what you deserve. What you deserve will be based upon the work you put forth. The farmer doesn't reap a harvest simply because he needs one. The farmer reaps a harvest because he deserves one. It's the farmer who puts in the time to plant and cultivate his crops.

We will not receive improvement and liberty simply because we need it. And yes, we do need improvement. We'll receive improvement when we deserve it based upon the work we personally put forth. And yes, we will deserve it!

Do you love America and what she stands for enough to join me and take hold of the plow? If you said yes, I encourage you to step up to the plate. Together we can stop the erosion of our American way.

We can't be complacent. We can't be numb. We can't be stagnant. We're either a raging river roaring down with great power and strength, or we're a stagnant pond filled with pond scum and disease. This raging river that America used to be is drying up and slowing down. It is time to turn the tide. We all have the ability to make our country the freest place to live once more! Are you with me? Great! Then, read on.

In this book, you'll learn why you and anyone who wishes to affect change can become a leader of both yourself and others.

You'll learn how to communicate without offending and how to persuade others in a non-threatening way. You'll learn that you can grow the Libertarian Party using these skills. I'll also explain why personal development and self-improvement are essential on the path to leadership.

Leaders are made, not born. Everyone has the choice to learn the skills necessary to become a leader and to work with others to advance the cause of liberty. The principles I put forth in this book will guide you, me, and all of us to the success, freedom, and greatness we were born into.

The Libertarian Party is looking to restore our freedoms. As a party member, I speak for myself and other members when I say we know you would like to work, we know you have dreams, and we know why you're being hampered by the government. ***And we also have the key to set you free!***

Now is the time to take massive action to reclaim the freedom that was once ours!

*"Freedom is never voluntarily given by the oppressor;
it must be demanded by the oppressed."*
~ Martin Luther King, Jr.

CHAPTER 2

THE NEED FOR LIBERTARIAN LEADERSHIP

"On the mountains of truth you can never climb in vain: either you will reach a point higher up today, or you will be training your powers so that you will be able to climb higher tomorrow."
~ Friedrich Nietzsche

As of October 2011, the Advocates for Self-Government's "World's Smallest Political Quiz" has been taken more than 18 million times online. If you don't know, the quiz is 10 questions formulated to plot a person's political position. (www.TheAdvocates.org/quiz) The quiz is designed to open people's minds to the truth that there are more than just two political parties in America. There is more than just left vs. right. There is liberty and there is tyranny.

The Liberty Movement is the fastest growing political movement in the United States, yet few people know what a Libertarian is or what it means to be a Libertarian.

I'd like to educate you now. The Libertarian Party has been around since 1971 and has been growing ever since. Its Statement of Principles includes:

> *We hold that all individuals have the right to exercise sole dominion over their own lives, and have the right to live*

in whatever manner they choose, so long as they do not forcibly interfere with the equal right of others to live in whatever manner they choose.

If most people believe in the Libertarian way, then it's time to vote more Libertarians into office. The key is leadership, both individual leadership and group leadership.

We must have leadership that can convey the message of Libertarianism in a proper means and format so the general population can see, hear, and understand. It's not that the party has not had the leadership; there just haven't been enough people stepping up and acting. We must have leadership from the lowest levels to the highest levels of Libertarianism working together for the common goal of liberty. With America on the verge of a complete and utter collapse, people are looking for something more credible, much more credible. We must let them know the Libertarian Party holds the solutions.

Right now is one of the greatest and easiest times in history for the Libertarian Party to step up and give Americans what they're eagerly searching for. The people are tired of the same, old, rehashed strategies that the two-party system has given us for so many years, strategies that have put this country into a state of confusion, fear, and imminent shutdown.

People are starving for something drastically different, and that is proper and powerful leadership. It is leadership by the people, for the people, instead of by the corporations, for the corporations, or by the special interest, for the special interest.

With proper leadership, the Libertarian Party has an opportunity to seize this moment in history and become the leading party that can save America and restore her to the grandeur to which she was once accustomed. To the place where the free market economy is flourishing, where ideas and growth are rampant. To the place where hard work and ambition can propel the average individual into the realm of greatness, into their chosen realm of prosperity. To the country where the pursuit of happiness is open to all, rich or poor, male or female, any race or religion, without government interference, as long you don't interfere with the rights of others.

The urgency for leadership by the Libertarian Party is blindingly obvious. America is in rapid decline. We're on the brink of an economic meltdown. Massive improvement must take place immediately! America stood tall for freedom against the rest of the world. She is now dwindling away as is evident in the comparisons with other countries.

This beautiful country has been beaten down by the two-party system that has delivered unnecessary and prohibitively costly regulations. This system has wrapped a rope of irresponsible runaway spending around the throat of America to the point of strangulation. It's up to us, the people, to take on the leadership roles to resuscitate America back to health, back to the greatest country in the world.

But where do we find these leaders? Are people born with certain characteristics or mannerisms of leaders? Are they born with the natural ability to lead people? Or are they taught to be a certain way by those who influenced them in their upbringing? Birth order, sibling interaction, parental messages, educational training, innate talents, all of these traits come into play when developing leaders.

Do most parents unknowingly teach their children to be dependent and inhibit their children's confidence? Have you ever heard a parent finish a child's sentence? Or have seen a parent complete a child's homework? Or clean up after a child? This may seem like help, but many moms and dads help a little too much. The parents justify assisting their child by thinking their child will appreciate the help and recognize what great parents they are. Actually, the child may be thinking: "Mom and Dad don't think I can do it on my own, so why bother?" Eventually, this parental assistance will destroy the child's self-confidence.

As children mature into adults, they'll bring with them this lack of self-confidence. Conversely, parents who allow their children the ability to be in charge of their actions and outcomes prepare them to be leaders later in life. Parents who raise children to think for themselves are raising potential leaders.

Regardless of how anyone is brought up as a child, it's still up to us as adults to take responsibility for our lives today. We can learn the necessary leadership skills and develop a strong emotional foundation through study and practice.

I'd like to introduce you to two levels of leadership that will grow the Libertarian Party into the force that will right the American wrongs: Individual and Group.

Individual Leadership

Individual leadership begins with you taking full responsibility for every aspect of your life. That includes your finances, relationships, physical and emotional health, also your strong thirst for knowledge, and your burning desire for personal growth. Individual leadership also plays a big role within a group setting because every group requires multiple leaders.

With individual leadership, you take responsibility for the decisions you make. You're either the decider in your life or your decisions are made for you. You choose! Would you rather dictate how your life is going to go? Or would you rather be told what you're going to do like a helpless child whose life is being controlled by others?

The reason individual leadership is so important within the Libertarian Party is because every one of us is a piece of the entire puzzle. We're each one cell of one body and a crucial part of one machine working to incrementally increase liberty. So, no matter what role each of us plays, whether we're as far up as the chair of the national party or we merely donate $10 a month to our local county party, we all play an integral role in the success of the Libertarian movement.

Group Leadership

A group leader is the professor of the classroom, the captain of the ship, and the person with the vision to unite a group together. Their mission rests on the ability to increase their influence to motivate people to action. With proper training in individual leadership, you can become a leader of others by default. Then you can mentor others to cultivate their individual and group leadership skills. Although not everyone may choose to be a group leader in a large group, anyone can be a group leader in their family and community, rallying those they know to the cause of incremental liberty.

What Can You Do?

You must educate yourself on the importance of leadership skills in your own life and focus on educating our youth, so the next generation has the ability to develop critical thinking, to ask questions, and to find solutions.

The impetus of responsibility is on every single one of us to get involved politically to improve the state of the nation! To make sure that we approve of everything our government is doing in our name. For too long we've left the control of our lives up to politicians who could care less about the congealing mass of people. It's up to us to learn how to take the reins and govern ourselves. Our leadership must be cultivated now while the opportunity presents itself and before it's too late.

If we stand up now and take the lead by educating ourselves on the principles of leadership, the Libertarian Party has the ability to be the largest political party in the United States. The dream of freedom is coalescing right now. In crisis comes opportunity. I truly believe that within every negative is the seed to an equal or greater positive. ***Don't you?***

It's time for everyone who believes in freedom to embrace Libertarian principles, to step up into a leadership position, and to lead others. You can start by:

- Reading books like this one on leadership
- Applying what you've learned here

- Attending seminars on leadership
- Adopting a "no matter what" philosophy, which means that no matter what happens, no matter what obstacles are put in your path, or no matter what challenges lie ahead, you'll make the Libertarian Party number one!

The future of the Libertarian Party rests on all of our shoulders; anyone and everyone has a responsibility within the party to be a leader. We must make the commitment to liberty before we're left with none at all. The definition of commitment is "elimination of all other alternatives." At this time, there really are no other alternatives, so isn't it time for you to commit?

We will succeed. We will retain our liberties. Keep reading if you're on board with me!

"Let him that would move the world, first move himself."
~ Socrates

CHAPTER 3

LEADERSHIP BY THE PEOPLE, FOR THE PEOPLE

"Fail to honor people,
they fail to honor you;
but of a good leader, who talks little,
when his work is done, his aims fulfilled,
they will all say, 'We did this ourselves.'"
~ Lao Tzu

America has gone from "leadership by the people, for the people" to "leadership by the corporation, for the corporation" or "by the special interest, for the special interest." What is "by the corporation, for the corporation?" Well, a state is incorporated and a corporation is a business. What does the state create as a business? Absolutely nothing. The real question is: Why is the state in business anyway? And where do they get their money? Do you really wish to know? They borrow it into existence from the Federal Reserve that creates the money out of thin air, by way of a printing press, or by raising taxes. Two main strategies, both are based on the printing of worthless paper and the passing it on to the public as real value. So, they either take the money from you by raising taxes, or they borrow it into existence and give the debt to your children and grandchildren to pay back.

Wow! How many times have you borrowed money and then made your children pay it back? Not too often, I hope. Now, one thing the state does create is illusions, such as the illusion of protection and safety! For example, how about air travel? In my opinion, you are not any safer today than you were pre-9/11. Yet your rights are violated, stomped on, and crushed every time you board a plane. I've heard numerous horror stories of how, every single day, people are intruded upon and abused unnecessarily while boarding a plane. Yet, guns and drugs are still getting through. ***How is this possible?***

You put up with all that revolting abuse because of the illusion of safety. Your rights of life, liberty, and the pursuit of happiness are in the process of severe erosion in every area of your life in the name of safety.

The newest one to steal your rights in the name of safety is the Patriot Act, an act that allows government to conduct searches without a warrant. Due process has been enormously affected, surveillance and privacy have been gravely altered, and indefinite detentions without charges have been brought forth. Various religious communities, political organizations, and other peaceful groups have been raided for constitutionally protected activities. All this nonsense is sold to you in the beautiful package of "safety."

I think it's a scary proposition when the organization that was brought forth to protect our rights evolves into the worst offender of violating our rights.

Believe me, if government is really on your side, then why are they doing everything they can to shred the constitutionally protected rights you have? Not only are you less safe, you're also less free! I find it disturbing that people will give up their rights for the feeling of safety. "Feeling safe" and "being safe" are two vastly different things. History clearly shows that when government gets involved, you as an individual are in most cases no safer than you were before government got involved, and you're also losing your liberties and freedom in the process.

Maybe founding father, Benjamin Franklin, was giving us a warning of the future when he said:

"They that can give up essential liberty to purchase a little temporary safety, deserve neither liberty nor safety."
~ Benjamin Franklin

Are we really a country of free enterprise? If you said yes, then why do you have to get a license to start a business in which you pay numerous fees? You have the illusion of free market enterprise. Many people believe they have a right to free enterprise, yet they first must obtain permission and then pay a fee to engage in the world of free market enterprise. If it's your right and it's free, then why do you have to ask permission, in the form of a license, and then pay for it? A license is permission to do something that would otherwise be illegal. Common sense says that if it's a right then it's not illegal. If it's your right, then you don't need permission from a government organization that can tell you, "No, you don't have permission." The words "pay" and "free" are polar opposites; they're definitely not on the same page! Therefore, "free enterprise" is not "free!" It should be called "fee enterprise!"

After permission has been "granted" by government, that entity set up to protect your God-given, unalienable rights, which has proved to be more interested in being the entity that takes and steals those rights, you then pay that same government upwards of 40% of the profits, "the fruits of your labor." The government entity that granted you permission to work did nothing to assist you with your work to earn this fruit.

The average taxpayer works approximately five months out of every year to pay their tax burden. Every day that you get up and go to work for that year, almost five months of that labor will go to an entity that did nothing to help you with that labor. ***Nothing! Not a thing!***

What did you get for five months of free labor? Would you give me five months in free labor? Would you continue to do that if your life was getting worse instead of better? Of course not!

When government has the ability to create unfair and unnecessary laws that prevent you from doing your business or that make it unprofitable for you to run a business, we as people and a nation cannot grow. When government can tell you how to run your business, by a set of rules that keeps you from competing with much larger corporations, that is not free enterprise.

And through the illusions brought on by the state, we, the people, have been pillaged and plundered with a redistribution of wealth from the hardworking people to the extremely wealthy and to the large corporations that give various forms of kickbacks to government. An example is bailouts. The government borrowed the money to give to large corporations and the people get to pay it back. The corporations didn't earn that money through honest work and ingenuity, but by massive government handouts of your family's money that you worked hard for.

Would you give a lot of money to someone or something that has already proven they can't handle money? Of course not! Anybody with sense would know you don't give large amounts of money to irresponsible people or corporations. That must mean that the government has no sense. But, they borrowed the money into existence anyway and gave it to these large corporations; the corporations did what was expected, very little for you and a lot for themselves, including but not limited to, dishing out huge bonuses to their executives. Bonuses for what? For being the morons who helped perpetuate the crisis in the first place, or for being the smart guys who had the government pay for their disastrous ways, at you and your family's expense?

It's chilling when government forces you, by creating laws, to do business with specific industries such as insurance companies or the medical industry (as in obtaining immunizations). It's especially disconcerting when there's evidence that suggests immunizations may cause more harm than good. Yet, the drug and insurance industries get very rich through government's law making.

Has the government passed any laws that say Americans have to buy what you're selling? Probably not, nor would I choose for that to happen. Yet the system is working perfectly if you're a beneficiary of the system. And who would that be? The large corporations, not the people. The people are the ones who pay for all of it. We see the vast wealth transfer from your hands to the hands of the corporations and the people who run them. "By the corporation, for the corporation" creates laws that unfairly benefit the corporation at the expense of the hardworking American family, and the result has caused many hardships in people's lives. This is not capitalism, this is corporatism.

Did you know that approximately 96% of Americans who retire do so ill-equipped for the years ahead, short of money? And did you know that 70% of new job creation comes from small business? More people would be able to support themselves, retire well, and create greater job possibilities if there weren't such an overwhelming amount of unnecessary government fees and regulations that hinder small business practices and create unfair competition that makes it exceedingly difficult for small business to survive and thrive.

"Harmony, liberal intercourse with all Nations,
are recommended by policy, humanity, and interest.
But even our Commercial policy,
should hold an equal and impartial hand:
neither seeking nor granting exclusive favors or preferences;
consulting the natural course of things;
diffusing and diversifying by gentle means the streams of Commerce,
but forcing nothing; establishing with Powers so disposed;
in order to give trade a stable course..."
~ George Washington

Corporate government has grown so big and so out of control that people are starting to wake up, and they no longer maintain the illusion of being free. Another example of having to ask for governmental permission is falling in love. That's right! You have to get a marriage license, which is permission from the state to marry. Oh, and it's not just getting permission, you also have to pay for the permission. If you don't, then you can't get married (fall in love), at least not legally.

The current system reminds me of old gangster movies I saw as a kid where the gangsters would force businesses to give them money to protect them. The only difference is that in the movies, the gangsters actually protected the businesses.

The government sets up random check stops all over the country to force you to show papers. What is this? Nazi Germany under Hitler's rule? Or Communist China? I remember once in California, I went through a random check stop. I saw police cars everywhere and a huge, police, motor home type of vehicle in the turn lane that separated the lanes of traffic going the opposite way. I incorrectly assumed there was a dreadful accident, or that they were looking for a murderer or something hideous. There were lines of police with flashlights going from car to car. Then it was our turn. The flashlight shone on the driver's face with a quick flash at the passengers. The police looked through the car, and then the intense interrogation process begun. I felt petrified, like I was in a documentary being filmed in a communist country.

At that moment, the cognition that America was no longer a free country was forever ingrained into my mind. The illusion of freedom was no longer mine, for at that moment the truth rang clear. Our great country is not what we grew up thinking it was. It is formed of one illusion after another.

How much are we paying the people in government to perpetuate these illusions? Do they think they're high profile magicians for our entertainment? Here are some statistics that should shock your illusions:

Rank-and-File Members

The current salary (2011) for rank-and-file members of the House and Senate is $174,000 per year.

House Leadership

Speaker of the House salary - $223,500 per year.
Majority Leader salary - $193,400 per year.
Minority Leader salary- $193,400 per year.

President's Salary

$400,000 per year.
An increase in salary was approved as part of the Treasury and General Government Appropriations Act (Public Law 106-58), passed in the closing days of the 106th Congress.

> *Sec. 644. (a) Increase in Annual Compensation. Section 102 of title 3, United States Code, is amended by striking $200,000 and inserting $400,000. (b) Effective Date. The amendment made by this section shall take effect at noon on January 20, 2001.*

Vice President's Salary

$230,700 per year.

I find it ironic that in the same year as 9/11, we as individuals were asked to cut back, in a time of crisis, while the president's salary doubled. To rub salt in the public wound, shortly after 9/11, the Patriot Act was pushed through. This travesty shreds the constitution and the rights of the people. It makes government bigger, more costly for the people, and extremely intrusive into our personal lives. The government has stated numerous times that we were attacked because we're free. The government has, therefore, limited our freedom, thereby allowing the terrorists who attacked us, and the regimes that support them, victory over our way of life. It makes more sense, in the face of tyranny, to gain back more inalienable rights guaranteed by our constitution, instead of less.

Our response as Libertarians is victory over terrorism without firing a shot. By empowering, emphasizing, and practicing the inalienable rights guaranteed to every American, we show our strength and unity rather than cower away from the threat of the terrorist regime or send more bombs that inspire the people we bomb to take up arms against us. If we, the people, lose our personal liberty, the terrorists win, again. If that's the case, then why did our government usher in laws to limit the freedoms of the people in the aftermath of 9/11? The Libertarian solution would be to gain more of the solution, not more of the problem as our government is currently focused upon doing.

We were not attacked because we are free. That is a false argument; it led to the "illusion of safety" our government procreates. Government distracts us from the true problem and solution with it. We were attacked because of government's foreign policy, military-industrial greed, and the average citizen's ignorant bliss that proliferates through never-ending war.

The assault on your freedoms brought on by the politicians, by the corporation, for the corporation, has been felt so heavily that millions of people are finally taking action. It's time that the efforts of these millions of people rapidly multiply and bring this country back to the great nation it once was. We must seek out, find, and associate with those who understand and love freedom.

That's the very reason for this book, to assist in the development of Libertarian leadership that will lead our country with truth and passion to obtain freedom for all.

Remember this: when you vote for evil, you can't expect anything less than evil. And the only wasted vote is the vote not cast for freedom. It's been clearly proven over time that both Republicans and Democrats have created laws that limit freedoms and expand the powers of government. By chipping away at our God-given, unalienable rights protected by the Constitution, one administration at a time has brought us to where we are right now. With strong leadership backed by real American patriotism and lovers of liberty, this country can and will be free again.

The American Civil Liberties Union (ACLU) wrote on their website, www.ACLU.org:

> *June 10, 2004. Resolutions have been passed in 401 communities in 43 states including seven statewide resolutions. These communities represent approximately 62 million people who oppose sections of the USA Patriot Act.*

When these 62 million people come together for the cause of freedom, at that time freedom will catch on and rule. It will be the leadership that orchestrates this movement toward freedom, and it will be the continued leadership for the people that will keep this country free.

Recently, along with 270,002 previous people, I took the Nolan chart survey which is very similar to the "World's Smallest Political Quiz." This survey was designed to help participants find out what political group they resonated with best. This was achieved by identifying which principles the person taking the survey believes apply to which political party. The results disclose the perception of the parties. Thus, the person can more accurately choose the right party for their own active participation.

The choices were Libertarian, Liberal, Centrist, Conservative, and Statist. The survey stated that the results are not in any way, shape, or form scientific. The site also stated that the survey doesn't and can't claim that visitors to their website are a representative sampling of the overall U.S. population.

The following information is presented for entertainment purposes only. Okay, fine, I choose to be entertained. Here are the historic responses to survey questions concerning the 10 topics below since the founding of their website in August 2007.

1. **Speech, Assembly, Press, Internet, and Property Rights**: the highest ranking was Libertarian, 69%.
2. **Guns**: the highest ranking was Libertarian, 63.8%.

3. **Homosexual Marriage** (or, as most libertarians call it, Marriage): the highest ranking was Libertarian, 45.3%.
4. **Foreign Policy**: the highest ranking was Libertarian, 48.3%.
5. **National ID Card**: the highest ranking was Libertarian, 62.8%.
6. **Trade and Money**: the highest ranking was Libertarian, 51.3%.
7. **Social Security**: the highest ranking was Libertarian, 67.9%.
8. **Health Care**: the highest ranking was Libertarian, 45%.
9. **Taxes, Spending, and the National Debt**: the highest ranking was Libertarian, 75.1%.

In every topic but one the people chose the thinking of a Libertarian. Not only did the people choose the Libertarian way of thinking on all but one topic, but second place didn't come within double-digit percentage points. If this was athletics, with numbers like this, a Libertarian would be the highest paid athlete in the world. You can take the Nolan Chart survey at www. TheAdvocates.org or www.NolanChart.com. Click on quiz or survey.

With so many people who believe in freedom and the true American way of life, you would think more people would vote in the elections for liberty and freedom, for the Libertarian way. But many people are uninformed about the party; that's why we require your leadership. I propose leadership as the catalyst in this book so that more of us can help guide the American people in the direction of their desires, which includes freedom, safety, education, financial security, good health, peace, and the unencumbered pursuit of happiness.

People must realize that when they vote with their heart, their vote will be cast for a Libertarian who delivers solutions for the life they're seeking. That is leadership "by the people, for the people."

Now, what does leadership "by the people, for the people" really look like? What's good for the people is good for the politicians. When politicians create laws, the laws they create are to further the cause for freedom. They are to encourage growth that allows every individual to have the same unencumbered ability to pursue happiness as long as they don't violate the rights of others. Governed "by the people, for the people" exists when every law created or every law repealed is done so with nothing more than the benefit of the people considered first.

Politicians must abide by every law that's passed for the people without any special treatments. That's right! That's the requisite change. Every law that's passed for you will benefit the politicians as well. When the free market is completely open, someone can wake up one day with an idea and be unhindered by ridiculous regulations to move forward to compete with the largest of companies. Good wholesome competition has always created better products in the marketplace, with the prices moving downward, and with higher quality products or services.

"By the people, for the people" means that you teach your children what morals are best to embrace, rather than the politically correct morals that government says you're to have. We require strong Libertarian leadership supported by the people in this country who deeply desire to restore their freedoms to make this dream of "by the people, for the people" come true.

*"The beauty of empowering others is that your own power
is not diminished in the process."
~ Barbara Colorose*

CHAPTER 4

LIBERTARIAN VISION

"Where there is no vision, the people perish..."
~ Proverbs 29:18 (KJV)

In the Age of Enlightenment, the rule of the monarchs, tyrants, and the oppressive church were challenged. People began to use reason and thought to direct their lives towards individual liberty and the free market. The origin of the word "libertarian" comes from the Latin root word "liber" which means "free." The Latin suffix "tarian" means "believer in." So, the word libertarian means "believer in freedom" or "believer in liberty."

What is Our Vision?

The party's vision is that of a unified Libertarian Party that is the largest political party in the United States of America. A place where we have a political system that believes in, and openly supports, freedom for all. To have the largest group of believers in freedom in the world. A system that allows every individual the ability to work and become whatever they choose to be. A place where economic bliss is created by anyone who chooses it, without an overburden of unnecessary regulations that hinder the average individual to compete in the free and open market.

Where we as individuals help and support the less fortunate, not by force, but by the freewill of the people. Where people are free to protect their families from violent crimes, without worry of prosecution. Where we have an open, competitive educational system that teaches our children the abilities to survive and thrive, in real life scenarios, rather than to follow obediently.

A place where your health is getting better instead of being in a premature decline. With freedom to select the health care of your choice including, but not limited to, a natural means of health maintenance and recovery, without FDA regulations that clearly favor the drug industry (by the corporation, for the corporation).

You must know it is wrong when natural healing practitioners with higher success rates than the average pharmaceutically influenced doctors leave the country, based on fear of what the federal government will do to them, because they use natural methodologies to help one's body heal itself. And I've heard it's actually illegal to cure cancer the natural way. As Americans, deprived of alternative treatments, we're now pressured to use poisonous treatments like chemotherapy and radiation, which actually only have an average 2-4% success rate.

> *A survey of 128 U.S. cancer doctors found that if they contracted cancer, more than 80% would not have chemotherapy as the "risks and side effects far outweigh the likely benefits."*

That's not hard to believe considering the power of drug companies and food manufacturers to perpetuate illness rather than seek a cure.

Our vision is strong for bringing the United States of America back to being the greatest country in the world, one that's loved and respected by all because we lead by example, not by force. **Vision is the most important attribute of a leader.** A leader without vision is lost. Vision is the compass that directs us all on the path we walk. We're either moving towards or away from our chosen vision. It's the distractions of life or the process toward reaching our desired goals that alters our path. It's vision that guides us back in the right direction. It's vision that unites us and allows us to overlook our minor differences such as race, creed, or religion.

Your vision is that burning fire inside you that lights up the path so you can clearly see in dark times. Vision is that unseen internal force that rearranges your reality to your perception of the way things are. We've all heard the saying "seeing is believing." I agree! So, I see it daily in my mind. I see it when I wake up. I see it when I go to bed. I see it at all times in between. My vision is so strong that I believe it as if it were already true; therefore, "believing is also seeing." Believe that we can teach everyone Libertarian principles.

"And Jesus said unto them, Because of your unbelief:
for verily I say unto you, If ye have faith as a grain of mustard seed,
ye shall say unto this mountain, Remove hence to yonder place,
and it shall remove. And nothing shall be impossible unto you."
Matthew 17:20 (KJV)

He didn't say some things shall be impossible; he said "No thing shall be impossible."
Whether or not you believe in the Christian faith is beside the point. When you're standing at the crossroads of life, vision will guide your way. In my experience, when the challenges of life are pushing strongly upon me, I don't focus on the challenges, I focus on the vision! I focus on the vision of the greatness within me and the destination I desire to reach.

I focus on the solution to overcome the challenges, while continuing to maintain thoughts of my vision. Vision is the difference between perishing and creating extreme happiness in your life. This is the secret to overcoming most of life's challenges.

The majority of people will follow someone with vision, because they trust they're being led in the right direction. That's why you must have vision as a Libertarian leader, both as an individual leader and as a group leader. Great leaders with solid vision can clearly see the direction they're choosing to go, while a leader without vision is controlled by random forces, like a small ship in fierce winds being tossed at sea. It's far better to control your direction than to have direction control you.

Vision also allows you to see further than others. The further you can look ahead, the more strategic and more secure a course you can chart. The greater and more detailed that vision is, the easier and sooner that vision will become a reality in your life. It's that simple!

The more people who come together working and focusing on the same vision, the more rapidly people will flock to that vision as well, and the sooner that vision will manifest. A leader must communicate the vision to others in a concise fashion and on a continuous basis. As leaders, we're responsible for conveying the message of the future to improve the lives of all. ***It's the responsibility of every believer of freedom to promote and support liberty.***

If every Libertarian reading this accepts the duty to share the Libertarian vision with just one individual; and if he/she helps that individual to also register as a Libertarian Party member; and if each of those new members does the same; in a short time Libertarianism will be the predominant political philosophy that people subscribe to and we will have the America we desire.

In 2008, we had 523,686 votes cast for the Libertarian presidential candidate. If each of those people reach out and get one more person to register Libertarian, we will have 1,047,372 Libertarian voters. When this trend continues every year, in six years we will be challenging both the Democratic and Republican Parties for the majority.

In seven years, we will own it with a far second for the next party in line. ***That is our vision!***

"A man who moves a mountain,
begins by carrying away small stones."
~ Confucius

America is looking for strong leaders with vision to help guide, educate, and support others regarding the personal and community benefits that come with freedom for all. If you prefer, instead of becoming a group leader, you can certainly become an individual leader who sets the example of what true freedom is for everyone with whom you come in contact.

Many opportunities are available to show your support as a leader. One is by donating money on a monthly basis; no matter how big or small, all contributions are welcome. It's the little bit by a lot of people that adds up to the millions of dollars required to support the infrastructure to achieve the vision we all have for a better life.

Make the commitment! Say, "Yes, I support believers of freedom." Many people over the course of history have committed their life for freedom. They gave us the gift of freedom. What will you do to restore it and keep it?

"You give but little when you give of your possessions.
It is when you give of yourself that you truly give."
~ Kahlil Gibran

CHAPTER 5

Purpose and Belief

*"Anyone can live heroically and successfully for one day.
The man who achieves a high purpose makes that day
the pattern for all the days of his life."*
~ Unknown

We're all born into greatness, but we're conditioned into mediocrity. People begin to become great when they discover who they are and find their purpose. They continue to work on it every single day. ***What is your purpose? Why are you here? Why do you wake up in the morning?***

It's okay if you don't fully know who you are or what your purpose is. It's okay if you're still looking for the answers to those questions. Let me ask you one more question: ***What if you did know what your purpose was?*** Do you think you'd wake up with a little more passion in the morning? Do you think you'd be more focused in your daily activities? The sooner you develop a purpose, the sooner you'll achieve it. Without a purpose, you'll accept mediocrity. With a purpose, you'll create a direct path that leads to success!

Purpose is the fuel of the fire that burns inside us. True motivation and inspiration come from a sense of purpose.

Purpose takes us away from the superficial and materialistic desires that have been programmed into our minds. We have few selfish thoughts and we give up living only for ourselves. A strong purpose will make us sacrifice for the greater good, enabling each of us to make a difference in society and perpetuate a long-term direction in life.

Purpose is the reason we're all here. Most people never discover their true purpose in life. As I said in the beginning of this book, *"It's my purpose to give our future generations a better world than the world which I inherited."* Personally, I believe this should be everyone's purpose. This should be the motivation behind all our actions. And I believe making this world a better place can be achieved though implementing Libertarian principles and educating others on the benefits of a Libertarian society.

> *"A man who won't die for something is not fit to live."*
> *~ Martin Luther King, Jr.*

What is Belief?

Belief is the foundation of everything. All things are possible with belief. Everything you have in your life, from material possessions to accomplishments in the past are all in your life because you believed them possible. Belief in Libertarian solutions will get Libertarians elected into office.

> *"Men often become what they believe themselves to be.*
> *If I believe I cannot do something,*
> *it makes me incapable of doing it. But when I believe I can,*
> *then I acquire the ability to do it,*
> *even if I didn't have it in the beginning."*
> *~ Mahatma Ghandi*

Belief is the psychological state in which an individual holds a proposition or premise to be true. A belief is built by our emotions, experiences, and memories. Remember, we can only think and speak what we see and hear. The details in what we see and hear, and how our past experiences and beliefs interpret them, create new beliefs or strengthen old ones.

Belief is intertwined and connected with virtually everything we do, from things as simple as brushing our teeth or locking the door at night to more complicated beliefs like political philosophy or religious leanings.

Probably the single most important factor that will increase your local party's overall success is your belief that every member can succeed in whatever they set out to do. Your belief in each member's potential is very powerful. As leaders, we must know and believe that everyone has the ability to succeed. When we act accordingly, amazing things will happen.

You also must believe in yourself. ***Do you believe in you?*** All beliefs start with the belief in self, the belief in your goals, and the belief in the outcome of those goals. A strong belief in your goals will come about by focusing on how you or others will benefit from the achievement of those goals. The pursuit of those goals will give you purpose.

No matter what obstacles or inner or outer resistance you encounter, believe that you can and will overcome it. We are taught at a young age that "practice makes perfect" and, while it sounds nice, it is misleading. Practice doesn't make perfect, it makes better. Every time you do something you get better at it. You are better today than you were yesterday, but not as good as you will be tomorrow.

Practice will give you confidence. People will imagine that your confidence comes from something real, because, in your mind, it is real. You see, most people will hesitate before taking action, even if action is what's logical. By having a plan that you truly believe in and by believing in it so strongly that it gives you a single-minded self-assurance, you'll be the focus of their attention. Take action by sharing your purpose with others, and people will believe in you through the simple force of your conviction.

So first and foremost, believe in yourself and where you're

going. Next, develop a plan of action and share it with others. There's one thing I'd like to warn you about. Not everyone will follow you, no matter how righteous your purpose may be, and some people may actually attempt to discourage you. It's up to you to stick to your goals and purpose with a "no matter what" attitude and belief. No matter what happens, no matter what people may think or say, no matter how you may even attempt to sabotage your own efforts, you will accomplish your goals. ***No. Matter. What.***

"If you think you are beaten, you are
If you think you dare not, you don't,
If you like to win, but you think you can't
It is almost certain you won't.

If you think you'll lose, you're lost
For out of the world we find,
Success begins with a fellow's will
It's all in the state of mind.

If you think you are outclassed, you are
You've got to think high to rise,
You've got to be sure of yourself before
You can ever win a prize.

Life's battles don't always go
To the stronger or faster man,
But soon or late the man who wins
Is the man who thinks he can!"
~ Walter D. Wintle

CHAPTER 6

BUILD A STRONG FOUNDATION

*"Alexander, Caesar, Charlemagne, and myself founded empires;
but what foundation did we rest the creations of our genius?
Upon force. Jesus Christ founded an empire upon love;
and at this hour millions of men would die for Him."*
~ Napoleon Bonaparte

***The ultimate goal of the Libertarian Party must be to
get Libertarians elected into office.*** Once a Libertarian is
elected into office, he/she is now in a position to reduce the size of
government intervention and increase personal liberties. These
are umbrella positions that encompass the majority of the stances
that Libertarians take.

In order to get Libertarians elected into office, however,
we must first build a strong foundation. We must put a united
organization in place that understands that the vast majority of
Americans will vote for the Libertarian message if it is explained
correctly, in a reasonable, effective way that is completely
understandable. The Republicans and Democrats have band-aid
solutions, whereas Libertarians build long-term solutions. When
these long-term solutions are presented advantageously and

appropriately, Americans will take the Libertarian lead because their solutions display more sense than band-aid solutions. *Would you prefer a temporary solution or a long-term solution to our current challenges?*

More and more Libertarians are being elected into office around the country every election cycle, and more votes are being cast for Libertarian candidates than ever before. The 2008 Libertarian presidential ticket received more votes than any other Libertarian presidential ticket since 1980. The time is now for the Libertarian Party to believe in itself and to believe in its goals. This brings new members and new money into the party.

Cultivate Leaders

I, for one, do not want to be running the party for the rest of my life. I have a family; I have other goals and dreams. With that said, we should all be working to build up other leaders within the party so that one day we will be able to step down because we will have been teaching and training others to take our place. It should be the goal of every Libertarian leader to train, teach, and cultivate multiple people as replacements.

Empowering members of the party to take on leadership positions give us a steady flow of qualified leaders to increase party membership, money, and votes. The leaders of the Libertarian Party are our sales force.

The leaders have the ability to excite the imagination of the people, even those with little imagination. Leadership comes from self-confidence, a sense of purpose, and contentment within. These qualities radiate outward in leaders.

Personal magnetism encompasses a multitude of traits, such as the attraction, self-confidence, and humility that can be learned by anyone with the desire and determination to do so. We teach aspiring leaders how to attract people to our cause with ease and very little confrontation. We teach them how to be successful spokespeople for the Libertarian Party. The leadership positions that must be assumed include National Chair, Vice-Chair, At-

Large Members, State Chairs, County Chairs, Ambassadors, subsequently, then, any position where a person is running for an electable office.

Develop Organizers

Many members of the Libertarian Party have no desire to lead but would like to play an active role in the growth of the party. These people are the backbone of any successful organization and they play a vital role in growth. They feel better suited for the organizational roles that capitalize on their skills in marketing, writing, blogging, administrating, and any task that doesn't include being a spokesperson.

Find out what people are good at and what they enjoy doing, ask them to do that, and they'll be more likely to stay active. Keep an updated, detailed task list so those who desire to contribute know what positions are available to them, what will be expected of them, and how much time will be asked of them. This will ensure more participation and better results.

"Treat people as if they were what they ought to be,
and you help them to become what they are capable of being."
~ Johann Wolfgang von Goethe

Recruit Supporters

A supporter of the Libertarian Party includes anyone who takes any kind of role, no matter how big or small, to promote the Libertarian Party. They may:

- Cast a vote for a Libertarian Party candidate.
- Donate money of any amount.
- Volunteer in a variety of positions.
- Spread the word about the Libertarian philosophy.
- Run for office as a Libertarian Party candidate.

Every activity taken to advance the party and liberty is a

valued contribution. With every vote cast, every dollar donated, every time the message of liberty is spoken, the party grows. Moving the party forward by taking consistent action, over time, will turn the Libertarian Party into a strong political force. Every supporter assists in building a strong foundation that will stand the test of time.

United We Stand, Divided We Fall
Yes, our primary goal is to get Libertarians elected. The end result is to reduce the size of government, to lift the burden of debt on ourselves and future generations, and to improve all areas of life including wealth, health, and relationships through increasing personal liberty. The Libertarian Party garners widespread acceptance by taking positions that benefit the people. We're a serious political party that people vote for. People desire more liberty in their lives. Increasing personal and economic liberty will offer greater opportunities for everyone.

The principles the Libertarian Party is based upon already have widespread acceptance. As the party continues to lift the blinders and show the American people that it is true to its principles, it's becoming increasingly apparent that it won't give in to the corporations controlling the leaders of the Republican and Democratic parties.

When polled, as we've seen in the Nolan Survey, many Americans believe in the same issues and platform for which the Libertarian Party stands. But, because of the media blackout of the Libertarian Party, those same people don't even know the Libertarian Party exists. Together, as a united party, we must spread the message; we must develop more credibility; we must bring more members, money, and votes to the Libertarian Party by building a solid foundation of belief in our cause.

> *"By union the smallest states thrive.*
> *By discord the greatest are destroyed."*
> *~ Sallust (Gaius Sallustius Crispus)*

CHAPTER 7

COMMIT TO PERSONAL DEVELOPMENT AND SELF-IMPROVEMENT

"An investment in knowledge pays the best interest."
~ Benjamin Franklin

There's an old proverb: "Invest a coin in your mind and your pocket shall overflow." What it's talking about is growing your intellectual capital. The more knowledge and wisdom you gain, the faster and easier you possess the ability to use that wisdom and knowledge to propel your life to the greatness you desire and to influence others to do the same.

One of the best ways to invest in your self is called "personal development" or "self-improvement." This includes anything that improves your thought processes and adds skills and knowledge. You can learn from books, CDs, and videos, or seminars, coaches, and mentors, to name a few. I've done some of just about everything that's offered in the personal development industry.

With effective personal development and self-improvement, you'll gain the influence and charisma that center around critical thinking, that is, thinking outside the box and overcoming obstacles. It's not something that is learned through the traditional methods of teaching at the government school systems. It's learned through targeted education, such as:

- By reading books on the subject and creating your own beliefs and style
- Through great mentors, seminars, and lectures
- By purchasing and studying courses on the subjects, then implementing what you've learned
- By constant application, trial, and success

With great intellectual capital and purposeful action, you'll be able to influence others to see things the way you see them, which is also the way that you believe will best benefit them. That's what leaders do. However, you must first be able to look at the world through their eyes and understand where they're coming from. Then you can show them why the path of liberty will bring the freedom and prosperity they and others are seeking.

What self-improvement does is to raise self-confidence. People with high self-confidence participate more fully in life. They take bigger risks, which in most cases creates greater productivity. They venture out into the vast world. The bigger your personal world, the greater the enjoyment you'll get from life. And the bigger your world, the greater education and experience you'll obtain. Personal development creates greater happiness; the greater the happiness in your life, the greater the influence you'll have on others. **As a leader, you must first develop and improve yourself!**

Good things flow to those with a happy, positive, secure demeanor. People who've been through self-improvement teachings understand the honesty factor and what awesome gifts that brings. Unlike standard politicians, great leaders tell the truth to their followers if they desire to encourage loyalty and to achieve results. When people work toward improvement, they're empowered to create greatness for themselves and others. The more people in a society who commit to self-improvement, the greater that society will be. And the more leaders we will have among the people.

It appears that education stops for most of us after college or even 12th grade for some. Yet, I see the education process as a continual life-long journey. The moment you stop learning is the moment you die, or at least your mind dies. If you're not growing, you're dying. If a flower isn't blooming, it's wilting. If you're not moving forward, you're moving backward. There is no standing still in life; everything's changing every second, minute, and hour of the day. Learning the principles and skills of personal development and self-mastery will give you the confidence you must develop to become a powerful leader. You'll undertake any task with the perseverance to see that task through to the end and to continue to advance past the conceivable end to greater and greater heights.

Personal development is a journey, not a destination. You'll find your success along the path of that journey because in this journey there's no end. There's always a "plus one," a way to one-up your current achievements. The education you obtain from outer sources will continually add to your knowledge base as well as stimulate you to seek wisdom from your inner sources. As you learn to go within for answers from your "Higher Self," or from wherever the intuition is sourced, you'll become even more confident knowing you always have a resource to call upon; it is available 24/7, without fail. And the answers you pull from within are most often the best answers and solutions.

Libertarians continually seek to improve themselves and others and to set forth the example of self-responsibility, self-creation, and self-knowledge. ***You don't find yourself; you create yourself!*** You discover who you are, then decide who you choose to be. ***You then become that person through desire, commitment, and action***. All three of these components are essential for success.

*"There is one quality which one must possess to win,
and that is definiteness of purpose,
the knowledge of what one wants,
and a burning desire to possess it."*
~ Napoleon Hill

For generations to come, citizens will benefit by learning the tools of personal development. Then, these may become innate. It's up to those of us committed to the promise of freedom to learn these tools ourselves, and then pass them along, for it's often said that we teach most what we must personally learn. We learn even more as we teach others. True leaders leave a legacy, a legacy of self-improvement to help create generations of successful people.

It's going to take all of us, you and me together, learning the skills necessary to correctly portray Libertarianism in a way people can understand and adopt. We must be able to motivate and inspire others to share Libertarianism with everyone they know and meet. It's going to take an organized group effort to reach the rest of this great country with the renewed message of hope and freedom. I'm absolutely certain that personal development skills are essential for us to strengthen our party.

I first started learning self-improvement skills in my early 20s. Having struggled through elementary school, I barely graduated from high school and had to take night school my senior year to get enough credits to graduate. And I didn't even attend college. Yet, I went on to create a successful life, start businesses, and become a great communicator and leader.

My turning point came when I turned 22 and my son was born. That's when I decided that I absolutely had to do something different. I seriously had to think outside the box. Deep down I felt there was something missing that was never shared with me before, never taught to me in school, never exposed to me. I was gifted with a personal development course by Jack Canfield called "The Success Principles." Through it, the world of personal development was revealed to me.

Personal development is a path that holds the belief that anyone can achieve their goals and make their dreams a reality. The Success Principles Course helped me to develop a thirst for knowledge, constant self-improvement, and the great aspirations I hold today. "I'm better today than I was yesterday, but not as good as I will be tomorrow." I recommend this course for everyone looking to create a better life for themselves and for the people around them. You can find out more about the course at www. LibertarianLeadership.org.

"There are essentially two things that will make you wise —
the books you read and the people you meet."
~ Jack Canfield

Some of the skills you'll learn through your pursuit of personal development and self-improvement are:

- The ability to minimize negativity and turn any negative into a positive
- The capacity to control your thoughts and emotions
- How to speak without offending
- How to listen without defending
- Ways to overcome limitations and overlook the limitations of others
- How to ethically influence others
- How to continually grow as an individual
- And so much more...

Improving Your Environment

Improving your environment is an essential part of self-improvement. It is one of the simplest, yet hardest, things to do. Do you spend too much time with negative people? Easy, don't spend time with them. But, what if those negative people are your family, and you live in the same house or have to see them multiple times a year at family functions, or they call you on the phone on a consistent basis? Then, you stand firmly, yet calmly and confidently, in the sea of your new knowledge. Be at ease with it by fully comprehending it all. Radiate awareness, peace and certainty. Not defensiveness. Only a firm sense of purpose. Stand with calm confidence. Then, you can easily hope that the real improvements you are making within your own self will begin to rub off on them.

Improving my environment has been my single most effective tool to advance my life. I started by changing the people I spent my time with and associated with or encouraged them to strive to be better, then by removing activities that "waste" time or are time neutral (like watching TV or aimlessly surfing the Internet). Any activity that doesn't drive me closer to accomplishing my goals or improving the quality of my life, I am omitting from my life. Replace your TV time with reading books and taking self-improvement seminars. Find a mentor who's a great leader and spend time together.

You will benefit greatly by creating a life-affirming environment, one that's in line with your goals of becoming a Libertarian leader. Every day you must make a consistent effort to inch yourself closer to the finish line.

You can start your adventure with reading more. Reading 10 pages a day equals 300 pages a month which equates to reading a book a month. Reading a book a month will put you in the top 10% of readers in the United States. If you were to volunteer your time or go to networking events, you could continue to meet new and like-minded people to introduce to the party's philosophies. Be as passionate and outspoken as Thomas Paine.

"The duty of a patriot
is to protect his country from its government."
~ Thomas Paine

These are some of the ways I've replaced unproductive habits with productive ones. What I've gained is knowledge and experience, assets that will always be with me and can never be taken away. I've gained positive, life-long relationships with people who have similar goals and dreams to mine. Because of the positive activities I've done and continue to do, every day brings new and exciting opportunities and people to me. My life is constantly getting better to a point that I now expect good things to happen.

I'm telling you this to show you that with consistent positive change in your environment, you too can have whatever you desire. Even little changes will make a big difference. An airplane that changes course just a quarter of a degree can end up hundreds of miles away from its original destination. Make a change in your environment now. Become a strong, powerful individual who'll make a difference in America through the Libertarian Party.

"Nobody can go back and start a new beginning,
but anyone can start today and make a new ending."
~ Maria Robinson

Personal development principles can help you achieve any goal, anything you set your mind to. They'll give you the creativity you require to overcome any obstacle, to find the solution to any challenge. Studying personal development has greatly improved my life and the lives of millions of people around the world.

Through this book, I share some of these principles so you can get a taste for what I'm talking about. You can start here and add to your knowledge with more books, seminars, etc. As you grow, others will notice your successes and ask you what you're doing and what you stand for. I know this because I get asked those two questions often. My responses allow me to frequently speak about freedom and Libertarian principles!

Get involved with personal development and self-improvement training. Learn the "Success Principles" and watch your life take off in all directions: better relationships, health, and finances, plus the increased ability to help others improve their lives and improve the well-being of our country. You'll be able to use your skills to advance the Libertarian movement to influence and impact the lives of the people around you. All leaders are committed to personal development and self-improvement throughout their lives.

CHAPTER 8

HEART OF A LEADER

*"If your actions inspire others to dream more, learn more,
do more and become more, you are a leader."*
~ John Quincy Adams

Leadership is a powerful position to stand in. Leaders are the courageous individuals who shape the lives of many people whom they help and support. **So, it's vital that we understand the heart of the leaders we choose to follow.**

Currently in government, we have leaders who lead for the benefit of themselves or for the benefit of other entities; they don't have the best interests of the people in mind. That would be leadership based upon power and greed. Conversely, you have leaders who lead to ensure freedom for all people. They lead to benefit each individual at the level that individual chooses to be at, based upon their ambition, drive, and fortitude.

People in America are waking up to the fact that over the last century our country's leaders have progressively worked more and more for themselves and for the groups and entities that supported them (by the corporation, for the corporation). This is apparent when we see that government leaders have many special privileges the normal American families don't have. These privileged few thrive under a vastly different set of rules. ***How does that happen when they're supposed to be working on your behalf, not theirs?***

And what about the enormous number of unnecessary laws and regulations that keep the average American from engaging and competing in the free market with large corporations? American citizens are looking for drastic improvements in their lives as well as in the leadership that guides it.

Now is the time for Libertarian leadership to prevail. Now is the time for Libertarian leadership that has a deep desire to improve the world and society as a whole. It is a desire so deep in the hearts of the leaders that they are willing to risk their very being to do what is right. This is the type of Libertarian leader we require, in each and every leader among us; one who loves America and what she stands for; one who can overcome the temptations of great power and greed, knowing that freedom has a price, and who doesn't cower down at the cost; who stands up tall, strong, and proud to embrace the meaning of America; who has the heart to see through to the freedom and liberty most Americans desire.

Powerful leaders have an insatiable desire to gain more knowledge and truth. They clearly understand that knowledge is the beginning of wisdom. ***They understand that the truth shall make you free.*** To gain more knowledge and truth, leaders become voracious readers of literature which propels their minds into the realm of higher level thinking. This allows the leader to have greater deductive reasoning skills and to solve complex problems. With extensive knowledge and an open mind to the reasoning behind why and how a problem arose, a prepared leader will discover a solution to correct a given situation much faster and with greater effectiveness.

Capable leaders listen to other people's ideas; they work together to quickly determine the legitimacy and capacity of each specific idea in order to discern whether to move forward with it or not. They have the uncanny ability to capture great ideas by intently listening to other people. Some of the most powerful creations and inventions have come forth from those who've been in lower rank positions. They listened. They learned. They stepped forward.

We can learn something from all people. Listen and have the wisdom to know when that golden nugget arises that can dramatically change your direction and ability to obtain the vision you hold.

Bear in mind that criticism comes with the territory of leadership. Don't allow yourself to take criticism personally. Some people are critics, so it's up to you to determine what is truly warranted criticism (feedback) or unwarranted criticism (attack). With warranted criticism you reevaluate, make any corrections, and continue to move forward. When the criticism is unwarranted, you continue to move forward as planned, ignoring the people doing the attacking.

In all things, love is always appropriate. Love is the driving force at the heart of all great leaders. The love for freedom. The love for helping people live better lives. The love of doing the right thing, even when the right thing isn't the most popular thing. Remember, many people believe the most popular things to be right based on propaganda or other delivery systems of misinformation. For example, television distorts the lines of reality for many people. I've been in discussion after discussion with some who've argued their position with such passion, yet have no real premise as to why they believe what they believe except that maybe they heard it from someone or somewhere. When asked, "Why do you hold that position?" most, if not all, people have extremely ill-informed reasons with no real basis behind them. Now I am not saying everything you hear on the news is a lie. I am saying to examine all of the possibilities and search for the truth beyond the media.

When leaders' hearts and visions are on purpose, they'll stand up for what they believe with unshakable fervor toward their purpose, a purpose built on a strong foundation with the correct premise. A Libertarian leader works on your behalf to deliver the liberty that allows you and our country to grow. A country will grow when the individuals in the country are growing. The laws of a country must allow each individual the opportunity to move upward without government interference; then, every generation that follows them will be in a better place than the previous generation. That is the mark of the greatest country in the world.

However, America, as we know, is no longer the greatest country in the world. It is indeed on the brink of collapse. There's a strong correlation to the ever increasing lack of liberty and the demise of this once great country. Past politicians have sold this country down the river to the highest bidder. The highest bidders have pillaged and stripped the rights and money from the citizens with help from our governmental lawmakers while portraying the "illusion" of safety. They have stolen from us. We stand here, empty-handed.

This is why the heart of Libertarian leaders is their compass to rise up and strip away the unnecessary shackles of burdens and inhibitive regulations that have robbed us of our freedoms. These are leaders who can look in the mirror without regret because they know they are working for you and for the betterment of our families. By putting five months of earnings back into the economy through the voluntary means of spending and investing, our country will be able to thrive again. By leading each family to success, these leaders guide this country back to the heights of greatness.

Libertarians aren't looking to achieve the same heights this country has seen in the past. We're looking into the future to surpass the apex of greatness this country once was. Yes, that's correct. The heart of these leaders will cause them to push themselves to do better, achieve more, attain greater heights. That is why our forefathers came to America. That is to be our legacy.

One of the main responsibilities of leading others is to help the people you're leading to improve themselves. You first identify their strengths and then build upon them rather than call out their weaknesses. Actually, you should ignore their weaknesses altogether. Instead, you praise them for what they do right and praise them for what they attempt to do. Life is one big learning curve. We're all born at the same skill level. Some have focused on improving certain skills more than others. Right now, focus on improving your skill at identifying strengths in others.

Most of us have experienced public humiliation at some point in our lives. For many, these memories haunt them forever. Releasing them may be challenging; you can do it. Being firm in your purpose eases the way. Being a leader isn't easy. Sometimes, we get angry and wish to scold someone for their weaknesses, but it's important to remember that no matter how angry we are at what someone has done, we should never humiliate or reprimand them in front of others. The best way is to cool down first and then address the matter privately. Speak to others at you would wish to be spoken to when you have made an error, as an adult.

There's no better feeling than public recognition from someone we respect. We should be constantly looking for opportunities to praise our fellow members. Always take advantage of any occasion to let others know they did a great job. Rewarding them in the moment is the way to encourage a great attitude and continued excellent effort.

Strong leaders are always working diligently to improve their leadership skills, driving themselves past their personal comfort zones for greater growth and power. Leaders know that when you push yourself out of the comfort of inertia into the "discomfort" zone of action for a long enough period of time, discomfort becomes comfort. With perseverance, hard work, and support from all Americans, we're looking to reach heights the rest of the world has never even dreamt of.

"Do not go where the path may lead,
go instead where there is no path and leave a trail."
~ Ralph Waldo Emerson

CHAPTER 9

BASIC LEADERSHIP SKILLS

*"The task of leadership is not to put greatness into people,
but to elicit it, for the greatness is there already."*
~ John Buchan

Great leaders aren't just born, they are also developed. Although there are innate leadership tendencies, anyone with passion for a cause can become a great leader. Look for those individuals in your local party, or find potential members who have leadership qualities, and help to develop them.

When becoming a leader, in order to know everything at the top, you must first learn it at the bottom. At the bottom, in the trenches, is where the development and learning process happens. It's where the fundamental knowledge is gained. Learning the basics is mandatory, and a successful leader takes the time to properly learn the basics.

In your journey to become a leader, you'll fail forward, get back up, dust yourself off, and keep moving. Everyone has heard the term, "trial and error." I've updated it to "trial and success." Keep taking different approaches until you succeed. When you learn the correct way to succeed, all you have to do is to keep duplicating your efforts. As you master the different tasks associated with being a Libertarian leader, you'll be able to teach others your successful methods.

Leadership Traits

Some leadership traits will be observable in potential candidates and some must be developed. These are typical qualities to look for in others and aspire to within yourself:

1. **Honest**: A leader sets an example for others by always being truthful, trustworthy, and open. Standards of excellence are high, and everyone is clear about what's expected of them.
2. **Confident**: An effective leader is decisive and confident in him/herself, inspires confidence in other party members, and enrolls loyal like-minded thinkers.
3. **Committed**: A leader must stay committed and responsible to the position he/she has accepted, to the party beliefs and goals, and to the members of the team. The larger vision for the liberation of Americans is always at the forefront.
4. **Creative**: A vital quality is coming up with creative, outside the box solutions, and tactics to get the job done.
5. **Courageous**: Someone willing to take risks, do what must be done, and not cower in the face of enemies and adversity. Someone who can lead others to victory.
6. **Cooperative**: Getting along with others, knowing when to lead and when to step back, and enrolling others as partners rather than as followers requires humility and high self-worth.
7. **Communicative**: It's vital to keep communication lines open, whether by phone, email, or in person. Teams must be kept current on activities that affect the members and the team's goals.
8. **Organized**: Leaders must be organized in their minds and in their surroundings: office, home, car, computer files, etc. It's important to return phone calls, follow up, and keep track of others' responsibilities.
9. **Motivational**: Motivating people to take up the cause and

enroll others takes a special individual. Great leaders have the gift of being highly motivated and being able to motivate those around them as well.

10. **Positive**: Staying upbeat, cheerful, and composed during challenges as well as successes sets an optimistic tone for the organization.

People Like Friendly People

A leader must be likeable. People are attracted to people who are friendly. It's much easier to like someone who is nice. Everyone desires friends who are kind, understanding, and caring. When you're the one who initiates the conversation and shows interest in the other person, you're building confidence and optimism in yourself. When you make a positive gesture to someone, even as small as smiling or saying hello, you're building up positivity in yourself.

In most cases, leaders are the most influential people in any organization. Therefore, it's important that you make your interactions with everyone as positive and uplifting as possible.

"If you want others to be happy, practice compassion.
If you want to be happy, practice compassion."
~ Dalai Lama

Every day is filled with opportunities to plant a positive seed in someone's mind. Most people have grown up in a "negative" world and have spent much of their life enduring others pointing out their faults. So, instead of falling prey to sympathizing or agreeing with their diminished view of themselves, be sure to build up their confidence. Inspire others to greatness.

When you're friendly to someone, they're more apt to listen to what you have to say. You also start the process of building a friendship and a connection which could ultimately develop into an ongoing relationship. By doing so you're building self-worth. The stronger and more abundant your friendships and connections are, the less stress and negativity you'll have in your life.

Being friendly will also help foster a greater sense of community. The Libertarian Party is a community. We must always be an organization with open arms where new members feel welcomed by a friendly face and a smile. The more welcome someone feels when they come to networking mixers, meetings or events, the greater the chance they'll come back to participate.

Not everyone is a naturally friendly person, especially in the world of politics. Yet, we have to strive to be above reproach, better behaved than everyone else. First, don't criticize, condemn, or complain, especially to new people. Always send your problems, challenges, or complaints up the chain of command; only send them to people who can do something effective or help you figure out a solution. ***Send your negative comments up and your positive comments down.***

Next, give honest, sincere appreciation to everyone involved. The Libertarian Party is a grassroots organization. We don't have big money or big media helping us out, so we can and should help to build up everyone involved so each one can become a leader in whatever means works best for them. Each person can and should help to spread the message and combat the big media lies. We can and should appreciate each person for taking the risks and making the sacrifices to go against the grain. This is the cost of freedom.

The last and most important thing is to make the other person feel special and significant. This is most easily accomplished by remembering names. Hearing someone's name is the sweetest sound to their ears. It shows you were listening. If by chance you forget their name, be confident and simply ask them to repeat it again. It seems easy enough, however it's very powerful. Also, encourage them to talk about themselves while you listen. We have two ears and one mouth for a reason, so let's use them proportionately. Find out about other people. Discover what's most important in their world. Do it sincerely. Enjoy it. It will give you the opportunity to practice for when you meet another person with similar concerns.

Apply Elegant Influence

*"Elegant persuasion is when the other person
thought it was their idea."*
~ Marshall Sylver

A leader knows that influence is not about getting someone to agree with him/her. You can argue, harass, and force people, but when they're no longer around you, they'll simply change their mind and go back to the way they were thinking before. All your efforts would be for nothing, so why even make the effort?

Elegant influence is much more effective and has lasting impact. Used properly, influence is getting others to ask you for your opinion and having them come to the same conclusion as if it were their idea. The art of influencing others is deeply rooted in emotion and in the subconscious mind. It consists of 80% emotion and 20% facts. Most people buy on emotion and justify with logic.

To be able to influence others, you must first influence yourself. That's right. You have to believe 100% that Libertarian solutions are hands down the best and the most effective ways to help society overcome any issue. Let's say you're standing on the top of a plateau, and you see a blind man running full speed ahead, and 100 feet in front of him is a drop off. Would you yell at him to stop? Of course you would. Why? If you didn't, he'd surely run off the edge and die. You would feel morally and ethically obligated to do so.

It's really the same with Libertarianism. "We the people" are running full speed ahead toward the edge of a complete monetary collapse, therefore it's up to those of us who've learned the truth to tell everyone else. Tell them in a way where they'll come to the conclusion on their own. That's elegant influence.

The goal is to start with someone who has little or no interest in politics and assist them to feel morally and ethically obligated to share what they've learned with their friends and family. Get them to the point where they tell everyone they influence to tell everyone they meet, and so on and so on. To reach this point, we must realize that the speed at which this happens depends solely on the ability of our members to communicate effectively. That's where it starts! The more effective communicators we have, the faster we grow as a party. To have more effective communicators within our movement, everyone must commit to becoming a more effective communicator. This starts with simply communicating, aloud, in person, with the people around you. Speak your mind.

Most people don't like influencing others because they associate it with coercion. They don't like the idea of having to sell someone an idea, having to convince others to think a certain way, or having to go through the discomfort of being rejected. They don't desire to feel like the Sunday morning, religious doorknockers. That's just so intrusive.

Yet, there's a simple explanation for this. The reason people don't like to influence others is because they're not good at it; they may not have any experience. How many people enjoy playing a game they're not good at? So, if you think you can't become an effective communicator and influencer, realize this: it is absolutely possible for you to become good at communication, and when you do become good at it, you'll enjoy it. You'll be working to save your country. **What can be more fulfilling than that?**

I highly recommend that you remember this: you're doing a great favor to everyone you educate and influence to become Libertarians. Unfortunately, the mainstream media ignores Libertarian solutions. **So, if you don't inform people, who will?** If now's not the right time, then when? You now possess the knowledge and the awareness. You are morally and ethically obligated to inform people of the truth. **Do you desire to save**

your country or not?

Now, not everyone will immediately buy what you're telling them. Realize that it's their loss, not yours. If they don't believe you or join you right away, it's okay. ***Persistence trumps resistance every time.*** You'll find that some of the people who hold out the longest will become your most passionate advocates.

Another, easy, productive way to improve your influence and effective communication skills is to upgrade your authority level. People in a position of authority have a much easier time influencing others. For example, as Northern Vice-Chair of the LPCA (Libertarian Party of California), I very frequently have people come up to me to ask for my opinion on a multitude of topics. They truly listen to what I have to say, even though I'm both young in age and new to the Libertarian Party. People assume I have a greater knowledge because of my position.

I'm going to encourage all local party affiliates to create a new position called "Ambassador" and to have as many ambassadors as they have people fit for the position. They should have an intermediate knowledge of Libertarianism and some training in communication and influence. (Training is available at www.LibertarianLeadership.org.) The last thing you benefit from are people who are calling themselves Ambassadors for the Libertarian Party going out and getting into arguments with people who disagree. Current Libertarian leaders should make sure these Ambassadors understand that their goal is to go out and build relationships which lead to voter registration. Voter registration leads to membership, membership leads to activism, activism leads to more ambassadors, and the cycle of growth continues.

With that strategy laid out, let's continue with some more keys to influencing others:

1. Always begin a conversation in a friendly way.
2. The best way to win an argument is to avoid it in the first place.

3. Show respect for the other person's opinion. Never say, "You're wrong."
4. Be sympathetic with the other person's ideas and opinions and honestly attempt to see things from their point of view.
5. Let the other person do the majority of the talking.
6. Use the "Feel, Felt, Found" technique (see chapter 11).
7. Focus on the benefits of your position and how it will positively impact their or their families' lives.
8. Use tools. Find videos that help support your positions and have the people watch them as "homework." Offer to look at anything they believe if they've taken an opposing position.
9. If the other person is getting aggravated, remember that in all things, love is appropriate. In other words, "kill them with kindness."

Voter Registration

"To be a successful political party,
and a competitor on the main stage,
voter registration, party membership,
and outreach must be ingrained in our culture.
Voter registration, membership, and outreach,
are what we do and we do it all the time."
~ C. Michael Pickens

The most basic task that will set you up to be a Libertarian leader is voter registration. Asking someone you know to register Libertarian is the best way to get the learning process started. Yes, the easiest and only way to register someone to the Libertarian Party is to just ask them to register Libertarian. The rest of the registration process is the fun part. Voter registration leads to party membership, membership leads to activism, activists become leaders, and leaders register new voters.

In the fall of 2010, while serving on the board of a Chamber of Commerce in Sacramento, I was asked to write an article on why people should vote. The article was to be used in an event pamphlet. The purpose of the article was to compel people to get registered and get active in the voting process. I spent nearly two weeks racking my brain trying to write this article. I eventually decided instead to write an article on why people shouldn't vote unless they were well versed in economic policy and had researched what they were voting on.

Some people look at those who choose not to vote as a cause for our country's ailments. I believe it's in our country's best interest to leave those people alone and not attempt to persuade them to ignorantly vote. Many of America's problems are caused by uneducated voters, or those who vote with only the persuasion of a TV or newspaper advertisement or the recommendation from a friend or family member.

If you feel the need to vote because it's your "civic duty," remember that your civic duty is not to just fill in ballots for the sake of filling in ballots. Don't vote out of ignorance, emotion, or to win approval from your friends and family. Your duty is to vote well, to vote in a way that at the very least makes the outcome no worse.

Every American citizen has the right to vote, but that doesn't mean it's always right to vote. Not voting can be a way of looking after the public good too. Not everyone has the desire, intellect, or opportunity to learn what's required to know in order to vote well. It takes energy. There have been countless exit poll studies done that show the average voter is shockingly ignorant about the main issues, the names of their local candidates, and even the policies that the candidate they voted for supports.

They go into the voting booth with little to no knowledge of what they're about to vote for, and within minutes of coming out have completely forgotten what they just voted for! No wonder our country is so messed up!

The MTV "get out the vote" campaigns aren't really helping one bit. But, it's not just the younger generations, it's all generations.

I'm not urging people to abstain from voting. What I am urging is for everyone to get educated about what and for whom they're voting. Don't let the advertisements and the mainstream media be your voting guide. Use objective judgment and principles as you educate yourself on all sides of each argument. Remember, there are always more than two solutions to any challenge.

"I would rather have,
one percent of 100 people's effort,
than 100 percent of my own."
~ Andrew Carnegie

When recruiting voters, start with the people who know, like, and trust you. This is setting yourself up for success. These people will be the easiest for you to register because they value your opinion, trust your judgment, and wish to see both you and your endeavors succeed.

A   sking someone to register as a Libertarian will start that person on the path to learning about the fundamentals of liberty. When they ask you, "What is a Libertarian?" always be brief. For example, you can say something like this:

"The Libertarian way is a logically consistent approach
to politics based on the moral principle of self-ownership.
Each individual has the right to control his or her own body,
action, speech, and property. Government's only role is to help
individuals defend themselves from force and fraud."
~ www.LP.org

In the beginning, stay away from going too in-depth into issues. I like to share Libertarian principles through videos because it's a medium most people are comfortable getting information from. The average American watches four to five hours of TV a day so it makes complete sense to dispense information in a way people are already used to. Additionally, video takes your personality and any bias a person may think you have out of the equation. You can find many great videos about Libertarianism on YouTube. Search for "What is Libertarianism?" Find a video you like, and use it as a tool to register people to the party.

Setting Goals for Growth

"Goals are the fuel in the furnace of achievement."
~ Brian Tracy

Leaders are excellent goal setters. You can only accomplish a goal if you first set one. Our party can't hit a target that doesn't exist. The first goal I set for someone who joins the party or wants to get involved is to learn about Libertarianism by completing the Liberty Academy Courses at http://www.LearnLiberty.org/libertyacademy. This is an easy, achievable goal. It gets the new member started on the learning process. After that, their new goal is to get one new person involved. And the process starts there.

Set your own goals and help your local party set goals as an organization, together. Find out how many registered Libertarians and party members there are in your county; set a specific and measurable goal for growth. Write down timelines, number of voters you plan to sign up, and what steps you'll take. For example, if you have 10 party members in your town, you can set a goal for each to sign up one person a month. That will double your membership quickly. Then, you can ask each new member if they can sign up one new member.

Make sure your goals are written down, with clear action steps and when you'll take them. Where will you find your one new member this month? How many people do you have to talk to in order to recruit one member? Will you do this in person or by phone? Do you have a list of prospects?

To be effective in achieving your goals, take these steps and you'll see your local organization expand in no time!

CHAPTER 10

CONFIDENCE

"One man with courage is a majority."
~ Thomas Jefferson

Confidence and self-esteem are by far the most important leadership characteristics you can have. With confidence you can advance your position in any situation in life. Self-esteem and confidence can also be construed as self-worth. High self-worth will lead to a more productive, purposeful, and fulfilling life. (Self-worth has nothing to do with a bank account.)

People with confidence and high self-esteem are able to bounce back quickly after difficulties or defeat and can look at these distractions as temporary. We all fight many mini-battles throughout our lives; our confidence along with perseverance allows us to win the wars. The more confident you are in yourself and your abilities, the more you'll be willing to risk being creative. The more creative you are, the faster you'll be able to find solutions to any challenges that arise. When you're more confident in your abilities, you'll have the strong sense of belief that you can and will achieve your goals.

With high self-esteem, you usually attract others with high

self-esteem into your life. You feel a sense of self-respect that others can sense when they're around you. When you respect and love yourself, it shows because you naturally respect and love others; you don't perceive them as threats that could hurt you or your purpose.

Having that self-respect will build you up and allow you to go through the day with less worry, knowing you can handle whatever comes up. You'll be able to focus more and to be more productive. When you feel good about yourself, you're more open to talk to strangers without hesitation. This is huge. Each new person you talk with is a potential Libertarian. Most people have no idea what a Libertarian is, so it will be exciting for you to be the first person to open their mind. I'm known for my ability to walk up to a complete stranger and start a conversation. I've actually built friendships with seemingly random people. All this comes from a calm confidence.

Having confidence in yourself will allow you to lose your ego and to accept criticism and feedback which you can use to improve yourself. Because of your confidence and strong self-image, you're more able to listen to the criticism and decide if there's any truth to it. People with low self-esteem easily shut down and get agitated when others criticize them.

One of the quickest ways to increase your self-confidence is by expanding your comfort zone. You should thoroughly examine your comfort zone if you're not familiar with what it is.

> *The comfort zone is a behavioral state within which a person operates in an anxiety-neutral condition using a limited set of behaviors to deliver a steady level of performance, usually without a sense of risk.*
> *~ White, Alasdair A. K. "From Comfort Zone to Performance Management" White & MacLean Publishing 2009.*

Within your comfort zone are all the things you know how to do, like to do, and are good at doing; you feel at ease when you're doing them. Outside your comfort zone are all the things that make you feel uncomfortable when you do them: tasks that are unknown and things you don't like to do, even though you know you should do them.

Comfort Zone

Tasks you don't like doing.

Tasks you are not very good at.

Tasks you know how to do.
Tasks you like doing.
Tasks that are easy for you to do.
Current skill set.

Tasks you don't know how to do yet.

Things that you are afraid to do based on non-physical fear.

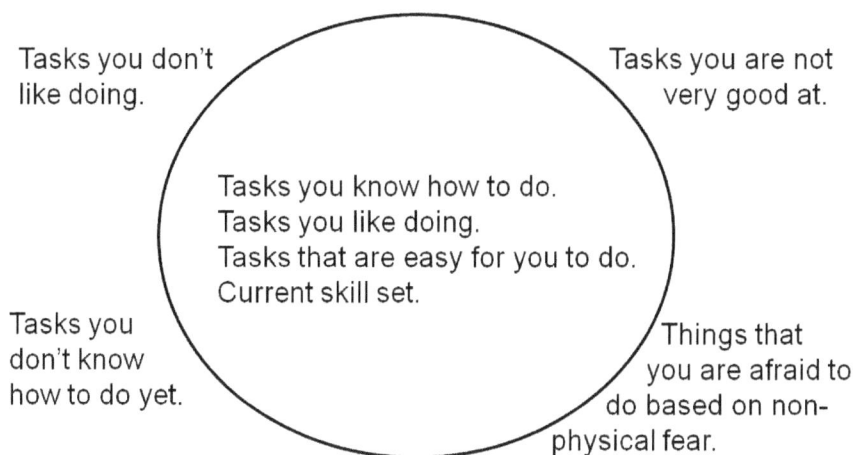

It probably seems like expanding your comfort zone would be a no-brainer. You would just do the things that are outside your comfort zone and keep doing them until you feel comfortable doing them. Pretty obvious, right? It is obvious, but there's a reason these tasks are outside your comfort zone. Just thinking about doing them scares you. There's a fake fear that holds you back. Remember earlier I said, "The biggest obstacle we must overcome to winning this war is ourselves: our limiting beliefs, subconscious programming, and self-created F.E.A.R. (Fantasized. Experiences. Appearing. Real.)." Most of the time, our fear stems from thinking we'll be ridiculed by people we know or that they won't approve of what we're doing when we attempt something and we're not good at it.

Have you ever seen a baby first attempting to walk? They take a few steps, fall down, get back up, and try it again. But, have you ever seen a baby take a few steps, fall down, and then criticize themselves for falling down? Babies don't make one attempt and then give up because they don't want to "look bad" for not walking on the first try.

We have to learn to take this kind of attitude and apply it to all aspects of our lives, to anything we desire to do but don't know how. Start taking steps to learn something new. You will get better. "Practice makes better." Practice doesn't make perfect as we were taught as children. When you say, "Practice makes perfect" you create resistance to attempting something new because you won't be perfect right away or ever. This can slow you down and limit you from ever expanding your skill set.

Perfection is something that's rarely attained. It's what we can strive for, although I prefer to strive for excellence! However, we should be content with practicing to get better and better. Expect throughout the process of getting better that you may fall down and you may make mistakes. It's only a mistake if you don't learn from it. When you learn from it, it becomes a lesson.

Take a golf ball, for example. When golf was first invented, golf balls were designed to be smooth all around. As the game evolved, the players found that the more dings, dents, and scratches the ball would get, the faster, farther, and truer the ball would go along its intended path. So, the design was changed to have lines in it, and eventually it became the way it is now with the indentations all around the ball.

The same is true for life. The more nicks, dents, and dings we get as we progress through life, the more mistakes we make that we learn from, the faster, farther, and truer we'll go along our intended path.

> *"Don't worry about failures,*
> *worry about the chances you miss when you don't even try."*
> *~ Jack Canfield*

*To learn more about confidence and self-esteem, I highly recommend Jack Canfield's 12 session course, **"Maximum Confidence."** This course has helped me take all aspects of my life to the next level and beyond. You can find the link to Jack's site on* **www.LibertarianLeadership.org** *underneath the "courses" tab.*

CHAPTER 11

COMMUNICATION: SPEAK WITHOUT OFFENDING, LISTEN WITHOUT DEFENDING

*"People don't care how much you know,
until they know how much you care."*
~ John Maxwell

Effective communication is the Libertarian leaders' strongest tool in growing the party. Learning these skills can make an enormous difference in the success or failure of the party to grow and to make the necessary changes to restore America her freedoms!

Speaking without offending is one powerful communication tool. There's no quicker way to end a conversation and make an enemy than by offending or attacking someone's position. In your personal life you'll gain significant relationships, and in the political arena you'll recruit more party members, when you speak with honor for the other person. If you're feeling challenged, take a deep breath, think before you speak, and look for what you can find that's good about the other person and their opinion. Sometimes it's a challenge, yet it's the only way to have a sincere, effective conversation.

Listening without defending is the other part of the communication formula. Be open to hearing other viewpoints without feeling you have to defend yours. I've often asked myself why people seem to want others to agree with them all the time. Life is more interesting when we can all state our beliefs freely, without having to defend them, and with the listener being open to learning something new. You might find out something you never knew before, and you'll learn a lot more about the person.

Have you ever put all your effort and emotion into convincing someone of the illegitimacy of the Federal Reserve, only to realize 10 minutes into the conversation that the eyes of the person you're talking to have glazed over? The easiest way to avoid this challenge is to ask the other person what issue they're most concerned about. If they respond by saying, "I don't know," ask them this: "Well, if you did have an issue that you were most concerned about, what would it be?" Most people will then tell you the issues that are most important to them.

Then, listen carefully to what the other person tells you they're most concerned about. This will build rapport and rapport builds trust. After you've listened to what they have to say, people will listen to what you have to say if they know, like, and trust you. *Listening is the key to all great relationships.* By listening, you show that you care what they have to say and that you respect them. "Hearing" and "listening" are quite different, though. We often "hear" the words coming out of others' mouths, but how often do we really "listen" to what they're really saying?

"Condemnation without investigation,
is the height of ignorance."
~ Albert Einstein

When you take interest in what's most important to the other person, you show you care. The quote at the start of this chapter is one of my favorite quotes on communication and influence. Take an interest in what's most important to the person you're looking to influence. You don't wish to be perceived as a crusader. Shoving an issue they're not interested in down the throat of an unsuspecting acquaintance, friend, or family member may leave a bad taste in their mouth.

A great tool for "active" listening is to ask clarifying questions. "Which part of that intrigues you?" "Can you tell me more about that first section you mentioned?" "What kind of solutions are you looking for?" People know you're listening intently and you're genuinely interested in what they're saying by the thoughtful questions you ask.

However, it's difficult to use active listening skills with those who are insincere speakers, poor communicators, or just plain negative people! While navigating the world of politics, you'll run into people who complain a lot and are very closed-minded. Most likely, they're programmed by the news media to believe a certain way. (It's called a "television program" for a reason; you're being "told" (tell), they are giving you a "vision," and you're being "programmed" with it.) My advice in dealing with closed-minded people is to skip over the issues you disagree on. Focus on the issues you do agree on.

The strategy you can use is to ask questions in search of common ground. The beautiful thing about Libertarianism is that both the Republicans and Democrats have issues based on our philosophy of liberty. There's always something we agree on. There's always a common ground. Let's celebrate our similarities and politely discuss our differences. Be the first to change the subject if you find there's a disagreement; be the first to agree to disagree and to move forward. You can "plant a seed," but don't attempt to grow the whole tree in one conversation.

People who believe a certain way have built that belief over a long period of time. Changing someone's beliefs is difficult, though not impossible. Changing someone's beliefs is utterly impossible if they don't like you because you spent hours arguing. Find common ground and celebrate the similarities.

Have fun with people who have opposing viewpoints. You'll occasionally come across someone who just desires to argue and disagree. They're generally pessimistic and confrontational by nature. The best thing you can do is disarm them before going into battle. The easiest way to do that is by giving them a sincere complement. I do that by telling someone, "I appreciate the fact that you've taken the time to learn about the issue because most Americans have no clue as to what's going on in politics."

I applaud anyone with a strong conviction towards an issue whether I think they're right or wrong. What the conviction shows me is true concern on the part of that individual. They sincerely care about America. Whether or not their opinion is misguided, at least in my mind, is inconsequential. I don't blame the person for having been lied to and manipulated by the media. It's the equivalent of blaming an abused dog for being afraid of humans. They don't know yet know of a better way to live. It's up to us to be patient, to show compassion, and to offer understanding.

Next, I have found a great tool that will enable you to convey your message in a way that's articulate and non-threatening. It's called the "Feel, Felt, Found" technique and it's a great sales tool. So, pay attention.

Feel, Felt, Found

How many times have you tried to talk to someone about a touchy subject and noticed they immediately put up their guard and had a closed mindset to hearing any alternate point of view? The "Feel, Felt, Found" technique is another communication tool that will allow you to quickly and easily create rapport and get the other person to relate to you. This is how you use it:

1. Empathize with them, and tell them you understand how they **feel**.
2. Tell them about someone you know who **felt** the same way.
3. Tell them how someone you know **found** that when they looked into all sides of the topic, they realized that the point of

view you're sharing is actually a good idea.

Here are some examples:

*"I understand exactly how you **feel** about that. I've **felt** the same way as have many others. And when we took a closer look we **found** that...."*
*"I know how you **feel** about the bank bailouts. I thought it was a good thing, and I know others **felt** it was too. Yet, when we took a closer look, we **found** that the leaders in our government were just bailing out their campaign contributors in the banking industry and getting paid off at the same time. Also, a bailout will hurt the overall economy by misallocating resources. When politicians grant special favors to a certain industry or a particular union, such decisions necessarily mean that market forces are being replaced by special-interest deal making. This type of interference with free markets is why nations such as France, Germany, and Japan tend to grow more slowly and enjoy less prosperity. But if America goes down this same path of government intervention, it's inevitable that we'll suffer the same fate of stagnation and higher unemployment."*
~ Example by Daniel J. Mitchell, CATO Institute

By empathizing with how someone **feels**, you're lowering their guard and building rapport simultaneously. When talking about how another person **felt** about the same situation, you're standing back out of the situation, thus decreasing emotion, increasing logic, and putting the person you're relating to in a place where they're more likely to trust you. Also, this makes them feel like they're part of a group, so they don't feel so alone in the conversation. When they feel like a part of the group, and you tell them how the group **found** out something that changed their mind, they'll be more likely to change their mind as well.

If the "Feel, Felt, Found" technique doesn't work, immediately change your approach. You may choose to end the conversation and pick it up at a different time. If you decide to keep at it, you can just go with the flow to keeping working at building trust by creating subtle shifts.

Here's what I mean. We like, and therefore trust, people who we believe are like us and who like us. When we trust them, we're more easily persuaded. We're also more easily persuaded when they don't knock our arguments. So, when discussing key issues, agree and shift.

Take a look at this example:

"That's a great point...and you might consider this..."

"I can see where you're coming from...and when you look at it like this..."

"I can see where you're coming from. Providing long-term aid to third world foreign nations is very compassionate to say the least, and I really wished it made a difference. For example, following a devastating earthquake in Guatemala, farmers trying to sell their surplus grain found the market flooded by the U.S. Food for Peace program. As a result, according to the Institute for Food and Development Policy, "food aid stood in the way of development." According to journalist Michael Maren, a long-time volunteer with such groups as the Peace Corps, AID, and Catholic Relief Services, aid to Somalia aggravated the country's famine, disrupted local agriculture, and turned nomadic tribesmen into 'relief junkies.' Similar results have been documented in countries as diverse as Colombia, Haiti, and India. Even when aid reaches its intended beneficiaries, the results are often counterproductive. Just as domestic welfare prevents Americans from becoming self-sufficient, foreign aid keeps entire nations dependent. According to one internal AID audit, 'Long-term feeding programs...have great potential for creating disincentives for food production. If Americans truly want to help other countries, they can best do so not through failed foreign aid programs, but by improving the U.S. economy, so U.S. businesses have funds to invest abroad and pursue free

trade policies. As the Congressional Budget Office recently admitted, 'Critics rightly argue that the broad policies of the major Western countries—trade policies, budget deficits, growth rates, and the like—generally exert greater [positive] influence on the economies of developing countries than does aid."
~ *Examples by Michael Tanner, CATO Institute*

And when all else fails...

*"When tempted to fight fire with fire,
remember that the fire department,
generally uses water."*
~ Unknown

CHAPTER 12

MENTION THE MESSAGE

"Having once decided to achieve a certain task,
achieve it at all costs of tedium and distaste.
The gain in self-confidence
of having accomplished a tiresome labor is immense."
~ Thomas A. Bennett

It has taken our elected officials 200 years to lead us down the road of government control and subjugation. Every president since George Washington has increased the size and scope of government. ***A little more government here means a little less liberty there!***

All for the good of the people, we're told. A solution to a problem. But, we all know that the solution to the problem is not more of the problem. We take an incremental approach to politics by offering solutions that propose a realistic vision for the next few years.

So, what will it take for us to dial back and to limit government spending and control? How do you eat an elephant? One bite at a time.

Our country didn't get to the state it's in overnight. It

won't be reversed overnight either. The public has been spoon-fed government growth at a slow pace to the point that few knew what was happening. Now it's time to enlighten them to the truth!

Would you feed a baby steak? No, of course not; the baby would choke and die. You feed a baby, baby food. It's the same thing with people who are new to politics. We have to feed them like they're babies. Give them information in bite-sized pieces they can digest.

When you give someone too much information or too many ideas that deeply challenge their beliefs, they'll choke and die (run away). Use a considerable tact and intelligence when speaking with new people. It took me some time to warm up to Libertarian ideas, and it's the same with some of the others I've spoken with.

Is this watering down of the message? I think not. Is it betraying our principles if we give our prospects information over time? No, conversely, it's creating bite-sized pieces they can chew, digest and be nourished by. In marketing, the average consumers have to experience something between five to seven times before they'll purchase. It's the same with beliefs. A belief is nothing more than a series of thoughts, emotions, and experiences combined to create a perceived truth. So, let's educate new prospects like we feed infants, focus on building long-term relationships, and give them information they can swallow in small doses. Let's build a healthy Libertarian body.

A Little Less Government Here, a Little More Liberty There

At a basic level, many Americans believe: the size of government must be reduced, the privacy of the citizens respected, regulations and fees reduced, taxes lowered, and war should be a last resort. These are all Libertarian positions, and these positions can very well garner majorities. These are the positions we should focus on. Offer these ideas to prospects by matching your information on the party's stand with their interests; practice the techniques I discussed in the previous chapter.

Most Americans would also agree with the Libertarian position proposing that individuals be free to make their own choices and to accept responsibility for the consequences of the choices they make. In honoring liberty for others, no individual, group, nor government should initiate force against any other individual, group, or government. That's an essential verb there; no one should ever initiate force against another.

Freedom of expression is another liberty most people agree upon, along with the opposition of government censorship, regulation, or control of communications, media, and technology. Recently, a proposed issue arose over the government controlling the Internet; the whole nation was in an uproar! The Internet is like the untamed West, one of the last bastions of freedom of speech and self-expression, as well as free commerce. If you didn't have a reason for joining the Libertarian movement before, this should certainly sway you!

Those in favor of less government are often those who desire the freedom to pursue any business freely. The Libertarian Party feels all members of society should have abundant opportunities to achieve economic success. A free and competitive market allocates resources in the most efficient manner. Everyone should have the right to offer goods and services to others. The sole role of government should be to protect property rights and provide the legal framework for voluntary trade to be protected. Any efforts by government to redistribute wealth or to control or to manage trade are not appropriate in a free society.

Another popular issue on which you can garner support from most Americans is the environment. They'll most likely side with the Libertarian position of supporting a clean, healthy environment and sensible use of our natural resources. Pollution and misuse of resources are the major causes of damage to our ecosystem. Point out how government, unlike private businesses, is unaccountable for a lot of the damage done to our environment and that government has a dreadful track record when it comes to environmental protection. In order to protect the environment, we must develop both a clear definition of and the enforcement of "individual rights" in resources like land, water, air, and wildlife. We must have free markets and property rights to stimulate the technological innovations and behavioral changes that will protect our environment and ecosystems.

These are some of the many issues you can mention in your message to potential party members and supporters. All of the main issues are available at www.LP.org, under Platform and Issues. The Statement of Principles of the Libertarian Party has been reproduced here, at the end of this book, for you to use. It is a valuable set of concise statements elaborating all of the main Libertarian principles.

Focusing on the Positive Will Bring Positive Results

When sharing the message with new people, you're apt to mention some of the complex problems facing our society today. Show them that when focusing on the problem, we create more of the problem. Share with them how we can focus on the solutions in order to expedite the process of reaching the solutions. Identify what works and how to create more of it. Enroll them by asking for their ideas. Discuss what outcomes are desired and what actions are preferred to be taken in that direction. For example, we don't wish to be anti-war; we choose to be pro-peace. We don't desire to be anti-Democrat or anti-Republican; we choose to be pro-Libertarian. As a leader, encourage others to become the solution by identifying the best solution and then taking regular action.

Practice Taking Consistent Action

By taking consistent action, we'll eventually reach our goals. Do one thing every day to advance the Libertarian Party. Talk to someone new every day. The most powerful form of marketing is word of mouth referrals. Everyone is a potential referral. Primarily, when talking with someone, ask them what they're most concerned about, and then offer the Libertarian solution. By understanding their needs and providing a viable solution, you become a valued resource. Then they'll desire to know more and eventually get involved.

We're moving the country in the direction of abundance, prosperity, and personal freedom. We know that to reach our goals, we must do something every day. As we all increase our desire for freedom, more people will come on board as they realize the benefits of living in a truly free society.

> *"The war against illegal plunder*
> *has been fought since the beginning of the world.*
> *But how is...legal plunder to be identified? Quite simply.*
> *See if the law takes from some persons what belongs to them,*
> *and gives it to other persons to whom it does not belong.*
> *See if the law benefits one citizen at the expense of another*
> *by doing what the citizen himself cannot do without committing a crime.*
> *Then abolish this law without delay...*
> *If such a law is not abolished immediately*
> *it will spread, multiply and develop into a system."*
> *~ Frederick Bastiat*

People Buy on Emotion and Justify with Logic

Sell the sizzle not the steak. Turn up the pain and bring in the pleasure. Put an emphasis on the benefits before mentioning the features. ***Features tell. Benefits sell!***

When I say sell the "sizzle" I mean point out the benefits. It's an appealing term in advertising. The benefits are the main reasons someone would choose to vote a certain way or back one of our issues. The sizzle will get them emotionally engaged, then you can show them the cow.

In every issue, there's some benefit you can use to get people emotionally involved, whether it will affect them personally or not. You can find sizzles in any and every issue. Find them and use them to get people interested. After you get the person interested in hearing more, you can bring up all the necessary details that will back up the solution.

For example: I hear Libertarians say they choose to

legalize drugs or end the war on drugs. Saying this by itself freaks some people out. People get visions of drug addicts roaming the streets, houses getting broken into, and their children turning into drug addicts. So, instead of starting the conversation with the ugly dead cow, you can start the conversation like this: "Did you know that Portugal recently found a way to reduce drug use by adults and teens that helped lower crime and reduce the rate of AIDS infections?" Then, when you have them interested in hearing how Portugal reduced drug use, you can tell them about decriminalization and all of the other features, 1 bite at a time.

WII-FM

One of the major issues we have as a society is that some people are very self-centered. How do you deal with that? Make all your points centered on them. Tune in to radio station WII-FM (What's In It For Me?). Someone who doesn't do drugs could care less if drugs were decriminalized. They believe that the law doesn't personally affect them. It's up to us to get creative and show them how it could affect them.

Creatively showing them focuses on discussing how advantageous it is to society to create the positive solutions and implement them incrementally. Being positive is more effective than the old fashioned way of using scare tactics to frighten your new friends into agreeing with you. Creating happier and more productive communities is healthier to discuss than the alternative of the necessity for more police force. It is more positive to say we are creating safe streets than to point out how much future money will be wasted on an excess police force. Focus on the solution, not the problem. People will return to speak with you again because they left feeling upbeat, excited and hopeful.

Some people think that most burglaries are caused by people who need to steal something to sell in order to buy more drugs. So, tell them that with more people recovering from drug use because of decriminalization, there's less crime and less chance their house could get targeted. You've just planted the seed of fear in their mind by suggesting that currently their house could be a target and at the same time offered them a solution to that fear. The seed of fear is the reason they are listening to you; the ray of hope in the solution is the reason they wish to speak with you about issues again in the future. Turn up the pain and bring in the pleasure.

How about the topic of lowering taxes? **What's In It For Me?** Did you know that when taxes are lowered you can keep more of your money? That means you can provide a higher quality of living for your family. At the same time, you're able to spend more of your money locally, and in turn provide more income for your local businesses, and therefore more jobs for your community, friends, and family. Lower taxes might mean a nicer car, living in a nicer area, and higher quality food. A happier family! Appeal to people's self-interests, and create a desire for our solutions in their mind. If the person you're talking with doesn't realize they require our solution, we'll make little progress. Just keep returning to the Libertarian way as the solution to their problems. Keep actively listening so you can offer the right facet of the solutions.

Keep in mind that the "sizzle" you offer for the person you're talking with may create a specific need in their mind. All "sizzles" may not be of equal importance. They may be important to you, but not to them. So, you'll have to fit each sizzle/benefit to the person you're working with. Always keep remembering to first ask your questions to find out what's most important to them. Also, you can gauge their reactions and responses to the issues you bring up. Work at seeing things through their eyes. This may take some time to learn to do; the more you practice, the better you'll get! Once you learn how to do this, you'll become a superstar at convincing people to join our cause! And you'll be able to teach others to duplicate your efforts, making you a true leader.

"A great leader teaches others to teach."

CHAPTER 13

VISIBILITY, CREDIBILITY, PROFITABILITY

"First, you have to be visible in the community.
You have to get out there and connect with people.
It's not called net-sitting or net-eating.
It's called networking.
You have to work at it."
~ Dr. Ivan Misner

I first learned about the Visibility, Credibility, Profitability (VCP) strategy while serving as President of a Business Networking International (BNI) Chapter in the Sacramento area. The VCP strategy was created by Dr. Ivan Misner, founder of BNI. This strategy is primarily used for business relationship building but can also be adapted to politics. To win a local election, you will creatively gain support from the local community. You do that through VCP.

Visibility

To gain support from people in your community, you must first be seen by these people. ***Start becoming more visible***! Attend and get involved with local events, fundraisers, and networking groups like Rotary, Kiwanis, Chamber of Commerce, BNI or any other local volunteer organization. Choose an organization with a cause that everyone can rally around without alienating anyone. Help this organization fulfill their mission and advance their goals.

Join these groups as a helpful citizen, not as an aspiring politician. Volunteer to be on a committee or help at events. Just being a member won't help your visibility; you must become actively involved. Start attending meetings years before you plan to run for office, if that's your goal. Take a sincere and active stand on helping your community. Your commitment to the community will be recognized, giving you the visibility, and ultimately the credibility required for a victorious and fulfilling campaign.

Credibility

Credibility is the quality of being believed or trusted. When someone trusts you, they'll follow you and take an interest in helping you achieve your goals. To gain credibility, first invest in your appearance. Like it or not, most people will make judgments of you upon first sight. It's a proven fact that those who experience success are generally well-groomed and dressed appropriately. Always dress business-casual whenever going out into your community because you never know who you'll run into.

There's also a direct correlation between credibility and charisma. Charismatic people gain credibility more quickly than others because they're extremely likable. If someone likes you, they'll take time to listen to you. The bottom line is to take time learning and practicing the principles of charisma. Read books about the principles of charisma and personal magnetism or find a mentor or a coach.

Build your credibility before you attempt to persuade anyone of anything. Once your credibility is established, the people who trust you will easily follow you and share their trust of you with others. You'll have a solid reputation of trust, community service, reliability, and commitment to the good of the community. Once you have credibility, you're easily able to become politically profitable.

Profitability
***Political profitability is measured by three things:
volunteers, donations, and votes.*** As we all know, corporate
donations corrupt democracy. Because of that, Libertarian
candidates don't take contributions from corporations, so
community outreach and credibility is key to accruing enough
donations from the public to run an effective campaign.

If someone trusts you and believes you're on their side,
they'll vote for you and donate to you. The great thing about
Libertarians is that we're not the lesser of two evils. We are the
"Party of Principle" and the "Party of the People." Even if you vote
for the lesser of two evils, you're still voting for evil. If you vote
for evil, does that mean you're supporting evil? If you support
evil, are you evil? I don't think so! However, becoming even more
positive by voting for your principles is an even better solution.
Let's become even more solution oriented.

Whatever you do, be as positive as possible in all of your
community dealings. You can't afford to turn anyone off. If you
get into a debate, ruffle feathers, or make a mistake, just give
up your pride and simply admit your errors. Keep in mind that
people respond more favorably to hearing the apology than to
hearing the justification for your error. Fix whatever you must
to get back in the people's good graces. I can't emphasize this
enough! More people will spread the word about negative events
than about positive ones, so you can't afford bad word of mouth.
Treat everyone you interact with as if they were the most precious
person in the world. Every one of us is necessary to restore
freedom to America!

*"The kind of corruption the media talk about,
the kind the Supreme Court was concerned about,
involves the putative sale of votes,
in exchange for campaign contributions."*
~ *James L. Buckley*

CHAPTER 14

MONEY TALKS

"All eyes are opened, or opening, to the rights of man.
The general spread of the light of science,
has already laid open to every view,
the palpable truth, that the mass of mankind
has not been born with saddles on their backs,
nor a favored few booted and spurred,
ready to ride legitimately, by the grace of God."
~ Thomas Jefferson

When I first became active in politics, I immediately became aware of a stark reality that is today's politics. ***To win races, the candidate with the most money is driving the fastest car.*** According to the Center for Responsive Politics, in 93% of House of Representatives races and 94% of Senate races that had been decided by mid-day November 5th, 2008, the candidate who spent the most money ended up winning. What did that make me realize? It made me clearly see that if I was going to play a major role in shaping the future of America, I would have to come up with some serious money. Also, I had to take into consideration that Libertarian Party candidates, unlike our Republican and Democrat competitors, aren't in line for any corporate campaign contributions.

Why won't corporations and special interest groups donate to Libertarians? The main reason is that Libertarians work to reduce the size and power of government. Corruption occurs because the government has the power to hand out special privileges. Take away the power, we take away the handouts. It's become common knowledge that those types of contributions are essentially bribes and that elected offices are for sale to the highest bidder. For example, elected officials, more often than not, vote in favor of laws and regulations that benefit the interests of their contributors. Libertarians, on the other hand, receive all of their contributions from the people and small business, therefore they move to implement policies that will truly benefit the people.

When solutions are stacked up next to each other, Libertarian, Democrat, and Republican, the Libertarian solution is the smarter, more positive, and more common sense solution. If this is the case, why do the majority of people not know about the Libertarian stances? That's easy. Again, Libertarian solutions do not benefit corporations; they do not benefit the military industrial complex; and they do not contain earmarks for politicians.

Since all of the major media outlets are owned by corporations, the Republicans and Democrats get millions of dollars of free advertising every day. So, why would the media promote a political party that seeks to give the power back to the individual? The answer is simple: it doesn't. The leadership of both the Republicans the Democrats seek to grow the power of the government, thereby keeping the power for themselves. The media benefits as it has a vested interest in that power.

As we grow the Libertarian Party in numbers, and our prosperity grows, we'll have the same financial power to affect change, however it will be for the people and not for corporations, media, and government.

CHAPTER 15

LEGACY

"A thing which I regret,
and which I will try to remedy some time,
is that I have never in my life planted a walnut.
Nobody does plant them nowadays—
when you see a walnut it is almost invariably an old tree.
If you plant a walnut you are planting it for your grandchildren."
~ George Orwell

What will you be remembered for when you die? Will you be remembered for your service to the greater good of society, or will you be remembered for your long stints on the couch watching television? Sad to say the majority of people will be remembered for the latter. The latest studies report that the average American watches four hours of television per day, also known as getting four hours of programming by the idiot box. Math was never my favorite subject, but when I heard this number I got very interested, and upset!

If the average American watches four hours of TV per day, that equates to 28 hours per week. Times that by 52 weeks per year, it's 120 hours per month, or 60 full days per year. That's right, two full months of every second, minute, and hour of the day for two months being utterly wasted. But wait, it gets better. Let's say you live to the age of 70. With the equation above, that's almost 12 full years spent watching TV every second, minute, and hour of the day!

But, let's be more realistic. We have to sleep during those 12 TV years, right? Let's add in eight hours of sleep per day, and it extends our television programming time, our time wasting, to 18 full years of our lives watching TV! For some people, these TV hours are spent playing video or computer games. The point remains the same; it's still just non-productive screen time.

I'd like you to imagine, right now, what you could accomplish if you could add an extra 18 years to your life. Now imagine you're on your deathbed and you're given an extra 18 years to accomplish anything you'd neglected to do. ***What would it be? What would you do with that extra time?***

The most common regret offered by people on their deathbeds is that they didn't have the courage to live a life of purpose. They gave in to social pressures: to fit in, to be a conformist, to follow the herd, even though we all know what happens to the herd.

Now imagine it's your time to leave your body. You're laying on your deathbed. Will you be laying there with regret, looking at the long list of goals and dreams left unfulfilled? Or will you be laying there with satisfaction at a life well lived? Will your funeral be a somber affair, where those who speak have to search for good things to say about you beyond the normal, "He was a loving father, she was a loving mother?" Or will your funeral be a celebration, a happy transition day, where your family, friends, and everyone you positively impacted will be reminiscing about all of your accomplishments and all of the lessons you taught them. Will they say you choose to lead the herd to better feeding grounds?

You see, life is short. Really short. They say that humans have been around for about 200,000 years. Since the average lifespan of someone living in America is 78 years, that means we'll be around a mere fraction of the time that humanity has been on the earth. It's up to us to make the best of the time we have here, to do the most good for humanity possible.

I find the best part of reading books and going through courses on leadership, success, personal development, and self-esteem is that once my eyes are opened to the truth, I can no longer claim ignorance. Leaving a legacy becomes a conscious choice. From now on, make a consistent effort to be, do, and have more. There's no reason to live a life of mediocrity and die with regrets!

As Americans, we seek a world of liberty, our God-given right. We deserve a world in which all individuals are sovereign over their own lives. From history, we know that the world can only reach this state by the people rising up and defeating oppression from within. Freedom and liberty can't be spread from the barrel of a gun, as we've learned from war. We must lead the world again, by example, not by threats and extortion. We must respect the rights of the individual, an essential precondition for a free and prosperous world.

The world we seek to build is one where individuals are free to follow their own dreams, in their own ways, without interference from government or any authoritarian power. We hold that all individuals have the right to exercise sole dominion over their own lives. All individuals have the right to live in whatever manner they choose, so long as they do not forcibly interfere with the equal right of others to live in whatever manner they choose. In other words, you own yourself. And as long as you're not hurting anyone else, you should be left alone.

Peace and prosperity can only reign again through freedom and liberty. This is the world we prefer to leave for future generations. What will your legacy be?

CHAPTER 16

ORGANIC GROWTH AND LOCAL EMPOWERMENT

"First they ignore you, then they laugh at you,
then they fight you, then you win."
~ Mahatma Ghandi

Governments throughout history have regularly operated on the principle that the State has the right to dispose of the lives of individuals and the fruits of their labor. Even within the United States, the government has been given the right to regulate the lives of individuals and seize the fruits of their labor without their consent. Taking something from someone without their permission is called theft. All persons are entitled to keeps the fruits of their labor.

Do you believe the federal government should stay out of the business of the state? Do you believe that the state law should trump federal law?

If you were voted into office, as President, would you make sure that state's rights superseded those of the federal government? Would you defend your state's rights?

If you answered yes to these questions, then you must also

agree that the Libertarian Party should follow the same principles that we're fighting for.

The Libertarian Party is doing a superb job of living up to the credo it has created for itself. We must continually monitor and over-communicate with our organization, on every level. This is true in all groups. Since we are aware of what hypocrisy is, we bear the responsibility to expand while exemplifying better principles than that. It is essential that, as we grow, we avoid the pitfalls of our predecessors in the two-party system. In order to rally the majority of the people to our side, we must maintain a political integrity unseen in this country for some generations.

The Libertarian Party is the shining example of proper representation, where the state party is guided by the county parties, and county parties and local members are empowered.

The role of the elected party leadership is to serve the people who elect them. Are you ready to stand up and take one of these roles? Have you named your own role within the party yet? As you read this book, did you envision your involvement, your next steps, your plans? What are your goals? What are your action steps for achieving these goals now?

It is our duty as leaders within this party to "practice what we preach" and to stand behind our principles. The state and national parties should be used as a communication tool, a unified voice for the county and local parties, and also as a collective unit that brings all of the best ideas from the different counties together, giving them a forum to make suggestions.

All politics happen at the local level. When we focus on increasing Liberty in our own communities, our neighboring communities will follow our lead. Focus on helping our candidates get elected at the city government level. When we have success at a local level, that success will spread to the state and national level. There is much corruption in Washington DC. Since the media tend to focus on what's going on in Washington, the corruption that is happening in our backyard is getting overlooked. In some cases there is just as much corruption going on in our backyard as there is going on in Washington. It is up to us to root out the corruption and to shine a light on the corruptors.

Solutions for Society
The solutions outlined in this book are incremental steps to improving our country and bringing more freedom, liberty, and personal responsibility back into the hands of the citizens. It is our pursuit of happiness we are defending here today. These steps are just a beginning. They already exceed the outdated steps that the Republicans and Democrats used to herd us. We are finding our leadership steps. We are making our own pathway forward.

We all agree that America didn't fall to where it's at overnight. It's not going to be fixed overnight. Our solutions must be articulated in a way that the citizens of this great country recognize as being the future and as being our rallying to our flag. We, the people who have heard this cry for life, liberty and the pursuit of happiness have already surpassed the state of inertia caused by the hypnotic suppression of the media; we have escaped the degradation of saying "No" to this decade's question, "Are you smarter than a fifth grader?" America can swallow it. *How do you eat an elephant? One bite at a time.*

Our founding fathers understood the suppression of an overbearing government. It is time for a new intellectual revolution to overthrow the suppression and oppression that have incidentally removed us from the vision of our forefathers. The vision necessary to guide this country into a prosperous future requires all citizens to realize the lethargy that has overtaken us. Though not with malice, the leadership of this country has stolen from us that which we hold most dear. That is, specifically, the freedoms of life, liberty and the pursuit of happiness. I cry out to you, fellow citizen, true American, join me in bringing this magnificent country forward to its greatness as foreseen by the fathers of this country. Awaken your hearts and minds! *How do you restore freedom to the greatest country on earth?* One Libertarian voter at a time!

Are you on board?

Please donate to Libertarian Leadership at
LibertarianLeadership.org.

Your donations will be used to create activist training,
focused on outreach, marketing, and Libertarian Party growth.

Be a Libertarian Leader now!

PREAMBLE OF THE LIBERTARIAN PARTY

As Libertarians, we seek a world of liberty; a world in which all individuals are sovereign over their own lives and no one is forced to sacrifice his or her values for the benefit of others.

We believe that respect for individual rights is the essential precondition for a free and prosperous world, that force and fraud must be banished from human relationships, and that only through freedom can peace and prosperity be realized.

Consequently, we defend each person's right to engage in any activity that is peaceful and honest, and welcome the diversity that freedom brings. The world we seek to build is one where individuals are free to follow their own dreams in their own ways, without interference from government or any authoritarian power.

Our goal is nothing more nor less than a world set free in our lifetime.

STATEMENT OF PRINCIPLES
OF THE LIBERTARIAN PARTY

We, the members of the Libertarian Party, challenge the cult of the omnipotent state and defend the rights of the individual. We hold that all individuals have the right to exercise sole dominion over their own lives, and have the right to live in whatever manner they choose, so long as they do not forcibly interfere with the equal right of others to live in whatever manner they choose.

Governments throughout history have regularly operated on the opposite principle, that the State has the right to dispose of the lives of individuals and the fruits of their labor. Even within the United States, all political parties other than our own grant to government the right to regulate the lives of individuals and seize the fruits of their labor without their consent.

We, on the contrary, deny the right of any government to do these things, and hold that where governments exist, they must not violate the rights of any individual: namely, (1) the right to life—accordingly we support the prohibition of the initiation of physical force against others; (2) the right to liberty of speech and action—accordingly we oppose all attempts by government to abridge the freedom of speech and press, as well as government censorship in any form; and (3) the right to property—accordingly we oppose all government interference with private property, such as confiscation, nationalization, and eminent domain, and support the prohibition of robbery, trespass, fraud, and misrepresentation.

Since governments, when instituted, must not violate individual rights, we oppose all interference by government in the areas of voluntary and contractual relations among individuals. People should not be forced to sacrifice their lives and property for the benefit of others. They should be left free by government to deal with one another as free traders; and the resultant economic system, the only one compatible with the protection of individual rights, is the free market.

1.0 Personal Liberty

Individuals should be free to make choices for themselves and to accept responsibility for the consequences of the choices they make. No individual, group, or government may initiate force against any other individual, group, or government. Our support of an individual's right to make choices in life does not mean that we necessarily approve or disapprove of those choices.

1.1 Expression and Communication

We support full freedom of expression and oppose government censorship, regulation or control of communications media and technology. We favor the freedom to engage in or abstain from any religious activities that do not violate the rights of others. We oppose government actions which either aid or attack any religion.

1.2 Personal Privacy

Libertarians support the rights recognized by the Fourth Amendment to be secure in our persons, homes, and property. Protection from unreasonable search and seizure should include records held by third parties, such as email, medical, and library records. Only actions that infringe on the rights of others can properly be termed crimes. We favor the repeal of all laws creating "crimes" without victims, such as the use of drugs for medicinal or recreational purposes.

1.3 Personal Relationships

Sexual orientation, preference, gender, or gender identity should have no impact on the government's treatment of individuals, such as in current marriage, child custody, adoption, immigration or military service laws. Government does not have the authority to define, license or restrict personal relationships. Consenting adults should be free to choose their own sexual practices and personal relationships.

1.4 Abortion

Recognizing that abortion is a sensitive issue and that people can hold good-faith views on all sides, we believe that government should be kept out of the matter, leaving the question to each person for their conscientious consideration.

1.5 Crime and Justice

Government exists to protect the rights of every individual including life, liberty and property. Criminal laws should be limited to violation of the rights of others through force or fraud, or deliberate actions that place others involuntarily at significant risk of harm. Individuals retain the right to voluntarily assume risk of harm to themselves. We support restitution of the victim to the fullest degree possible at the expense of the criminal or the negligent wrongdoer. We oppose reduction of constitutional safeguards of the rights of the criminally accused. The rights of due process, a speedy trial, legal counsel, trial by jury, and the legal presumption of innocence until proven guilty, must not be denied. We assert the common-law right of juries to judge not only the facts but also the justice of the law.

1.6 Self-Defense

The only legitimate use of force is in defense of individual rights — life, liberty, and justly acquired property — against aggression. This right inheres in the individual, who may agree to be aided by any other individual or group. We affirm the individual right recognized by the Second Amendment to keep and bear arms, and oppose the prosecution of individuals for exercising their rights of self-defense. We oppose all laws at any level of government requiring registration of, or restricting, the ownership, manufacture, or transfer or sale of firearms or ammunition.

2.0 Economic Liberty

Libertarians want all members of society to have abundant opportunities to achieve economic success. A free and competitive market allocates resources in the most efficient manner. Each person has the right to offer goods and services to others on the free market. The only proper role of government in the economic realm is to protect property rights, adjudicate disputes, and provide a legal framework in which voluntary trade is protected. All efforts by government to redistribute wealth, or to control or manage trade, are improper in a free society.

2.1 Property and Contract

Property rights are entitled to the same protection as all other human rights. The owners of property have the full right to control, use, dispose of, or in any manner enjoy, their property without interference, until and unless the exercise of their control infringes the valid rights of others. We oppose all controls on wages, prices, rents, profits, production, and interest rates. We advocate the repeal of all laws banning or restricting the advertising of prices, products, or services. We oppose all violations of the right to private property, liberty of contract, and freedom of trade. The right to trade includes the right not to trade — for any reasons whatsoever. Where property, including land, has been taken from its rightful owners by the government or private action in violation of individual rights, we favor restitution to the rightful owners.

2.2 Environment

We support a clean and healthy environment and sensible use of our natural resources. Private landowners and conservation groups have a vested interest in maintaining natural resources. Pollution and misuse of resources cause damage to our ecosystem. Governments, unlike private businesses, are unaccountable for such damage done to our environment and have a terrible track record when it comes to environmental protection. Protecting the environment requires a clear definition and enforcement of individual rights in resources like land, water, air, and wildlife. Free markets and property rights stimulate the technological innovations and behavioral changes required to protect our environment and ecosystems. We realize that our planet's climate is constantly changing, but environmental advocates and social pressure are the most effective means of changing public behavior.

2.3 Energy and Resources

While energy is needed to fuel a modern society, government should not be subsidizing any particular form of energy. We oppose all government control of energy pricing, allocation, and production.

2.4 Government Finance and Spending

All persons are entitled to keep the fruits of their labor. We call for the repeal of the income tax, the abolishment of the Internal Revenue Service and all federal programs and services not required under the U.S. Constitution. We oppose any legal requirements forcing employers to serve as tax collectors. Government should not incur debt, which burdens future generations without their consent. We support the passage of a "Balanced Budget Amendment" to the U.S. Constitution, provided that the budget is balanced exclusively by cutting expenditures, and not by raising taxes.

2.5 Money and Financial Markets

We favor free-market banking, with unrestricted competition among banks and depository institutions of all types. Individuals engaged in voluntary exchange should be free to use as money any mutually agreeable commodity or item. We support a halt to inflationary monetary policies and unconstitutional legal tender laws.

2.6 Monopolies and Corporations

We defend the right of individuals to form corporations, cooperatives and other types of companies based on voluntary association. We seek to divest government of all functions that can be provided by non-governmental organizations or private individuals. We oppose government subsidies to business, labor, or any other special interest. Industries should be governed by free markets.

2.7 Labor Markets

We support repeal of all laws which impede the ability of any person to find employment. We oppose government-fostered forced retirement. We support the right of free persons to associate or not associate in labor unions, and an employer should have the right to recognize or refuse to recognize a union. We oppose government interference in bargaining, such as compulsory arbitration or imposing an obligation to bargain.

2.8 Education

Education, like any other service, is best provided by the free market, achieving greater quality and efficiency with more diversity of choice. Schools should be managed locally to achieve greater accountability and parental involvement. Recognizing that the education of children is inextricably linked to moral values, we would return authority to parents to determine the education of their children, without interference from government. In particular, parents should have control of and responsibility for all funds expended for their children's education.

2.9   Health Care

We favor restoring and reviving a free market health care system. We recognize the freedom of individuals to determine the level of health insurance they want, the level of health care they want, the care providers they want, the medicines and treatments they will use and all other aspects of their medical care, including end-of-life decisions. People should be free to purchase health insurance across state lines.

2.10   Retirement and Income Security

Retirement planning is the responsibility of the individual, not the government. Libertarians would phase out the current government-sponsored Social Security system and transition to a private voluntary system. The proper and most effective source of help for the poor is the voluntary efforts of private groups and individuals. We believe members of society will become more charitable and civil society will be strengthened as government reduces its activity in this realm.

3.0   Securing Liberty

The protection of individual rights is the only proper purpose of government. Government is constitutionally limited so as to prevent the infringement of individual rights by the government itself. The principle of non-initiation of force should guide the relationships between governments.

3.1 National Defense

We support the maintenance of a sufficient military to defend the United States against aggression. The United States should both avoid entangling alliances and abandon its attempts to act as policeman for the world. We oppose any form of compulsory national service.

3.2 Internal Security and Individual Rights

The defense of the country requires that we have adequate intelligence to detect and to counter threats to domestic security. This requirement must not take priority over maintaining the civil liberties of our citizens. The Constitution and Bill of Rights shall not be suspended even during time of war. Intelligence agencies that legitimately seek to preserve the security of the nation must be subject to oversight and transparency. We oppose the government's use of secret classifications to keep from the public information that it should have, especially that which shows that the government has violated the law.

3.3 International Affairs

American foreign policy should seek an America at peace with the world. Our foreign policy should emphasize defense against attack from abroad and enhance the likelihood of peace by avoiding foreign entanglements. We would end the current U.S. government policy of foreign intervention, including military and economic aid. We recognize the right of all people to resist tyranny and defend themselves and their rights. We condemn the use of force, and especially the use of terrorism, against the innocent, regardless of whether such acts are committed by governments or by political or revolutionary groups.

3.4   Free Trade and Migration

We support the removal of governmental impediments to free trade. Political freedom and escape from tyranny demand that individuals not be unreasonably constrained by government in the crossing of political boundaries. Economic freedom demands the unrestricted movement of human as well as financial capital across national borders. However, we support control over the entry into our country of foreign nationals who pose a credible threat to security, health or property.

3.5   Rights and Discrimination

We condemn bigotry as irrational and repugnant. Government should not deny or abridge any individual's rights based on sex, wealth, race, color, creed, age, national origin, personal habits, political preference or sexual orientation. Parents, or other guardians, have the right to raise their children according to their own standards and beliefs.

3.6   Representative Government

We support electoral systems that are more representative of the electorate at the federal, state and local levels. As private voluntary groups, political parties should be allowed to establish their own rules for nomination procedures, primaries and conventions. We call for an end to any tax-financed subsidies to candidates or parties and the repeal of all laws which restrict voluntary financing of election campaigns. We oppose laws that effectively exclude alternative candidates and parties, deny ballot access, gerrymander districts, or deny the voters their right to consider all legitimate alternatives.

3.7   Self-Determination

Whenever any form of government becomes destructive of individual liberty, it is the right of the people to alter or to abolish it, and to agree to such new governance as to them shall seem most likely to protect their liberty.

4.0   Omissions

Our silence about any other particular government law, regulation, ordinance, directive, edict, control, regulatory agency, activity, or machination should not be construed to imply approval.

RESTORING LEGISLATIVE REPRESENTATION

By Michael Warnken,
Executive Director, Project Commonwealth
www.ProjectCommonwealth.com

It is clear to us that our American government is becoming more and more oppressive as time goes by. We are often aghast at articles we read almost daily documenting corruption and how our civil liberties are being infringed on and ground into oblivion by government at all levels.

We have become disillusioned by the electoral process. Elections are won regularly by the candidates who raise the most money; overwhelmingly, these are the incumbents. It's generally the case that huge corporations and even government agencies or their employees control elections. Their contributions to the electoral process, in either money or manpower, seem to be simple payoffs to extend their control over the victor. We also see the benefits and kickbacks given to these groups after the elections.

Incumbents rarely lose. Money clearly contributes to the low rate of turnover. Even when term limits are added into the equation, the machine seems to be able to find someone who can grab the mantle and get elected over someone who is a bona fide reformer or third party candidate.

Even those few true reformers who do get elected tend to get corrupted by the process. Their reforms never seem to gain any traction or get implemented. Those very few reforms which are implemented are often toothless, complicated, or have many loopholes, or are so lacking in enforcement clauses as to make them mockeries. When those reforms involve the creation of new agencies, those agencies become ongoing bureaucracies that are often co-opted by the very entities that they were intended to oversee and begin to protect what they were created to check.

So, the question that so many of us are asking, but never seem to have answered, is: how do we change all of this? Are we to be forever caught in this endless cycle, or is there a way out?

Civil Libertarians can identify when and how our rights are being taken such as the recent passage of NDAA and other such similar laws, but they often do not realize that the root cause of the denigration of our rights can be directly traced to the structure of our government. In order for Libertarians (and the rest of us) to have the freedoms that they espouse, our government must be formed in such a way as to promote liberty. Even the American founders noted that just placing liberties in writing was not enough.

The biggest problem in government, and the reason we have all the problems that we do, is our lack of representation in the legislative branch of government at almost every level of government, from federal to state to local.

As the population of America grows, the district size for each legislative representative grows. This is primarily due to the fact that we do not increase the number of representatives. As these districts grow, the representatives become increasingly divorced from their constituents. Other influences outside the citizens themselves begin take hold of the process, and the citizens begin to lose the very anchor to retaining their rights.[1] These rights will continue to erode unless something is done to stop this.

Sam Adams noted that the creation of the representative body was of the utmost importance and great care should be used

---

1   "When the ratio of representation rises to the level where the officeholder's primary loyalty no longer lies with the electorate, this justification of democratic systems becomes less compelling. Thus, an adequate ratio of representation serves as more than just a check on the representatives—it also represents a key component of mainstream theories of democratic legitimacy." Christopher Straw, The Role of Electoral Accountability, (New York: Journal of Legislation and Public Policy, 2008), Vol. 11:321, p. 355.

in its creation.[2] Thomas Paine noted the importance of having a representative body when it is no longer convenient for all citizens in a polity to meet. He then noted the importance for that representation to increase as the population increases.[3] We have not attended to these ideals as representation, in most cases, has not increased in some places for a very long time. In other cases, representation has not increased at all. It is generally the case that we have no substantive representation whatsoever! An examination of representation at each level of government needs very long time. In other cases, representation has not increased at all. It is generally the case that we have no substantive representation whatsoever! An examination of representation at each level of government needs to be made.

I. FEDERAL REPRESENTATION

A. The Size of the U.S. House
1. How It Began
The design of the federal legislature was established in the Constitutional Convention of 1787. Congress was divided into two chambers, the House and the Senate. The House was to represent the interests of the national citizenry in the state they were elected from. The senators were to be elected by the state

---

2   "The principal difficulty lies, and the greatest care should be employed in constituting this Representative Assembly. It should be in miniature, an exact portrait of the people at large. It should think, feel, reason, and act like them. That it may be the interest of this Assembly to do strict justice at all times, it should be an equal representation, or in other words equal interest among the people should have equal interest in it." Edited by Robert J. Taylor et al., Papers of John Adams, (Cambridge: Belknap Press of Harvard University Press, 1977).
3   "Some convenient tree will afford them a State-House, under the branches of which, the whole colony may assemble to deliberate on public matters. It is more than probable that their first laws will have the title only of Regulations, and be enforced by no other penalty than public disesteem. In this first parliament every man, by natural right will have a seat.
But as the colony increases, the public concerns will increase likewise, and the distance at which the members may be separated, will render it too inconvenient for all of them to meet on every occasion as at first, when their number was small, their habitations near, and the public concerns few and trifling. This will point out the convenience of their consenting to leave the legislative part to be managed by a select number chosen from the whole body, who are supposed to have the same concerns at stake which those have who appointed them, and who will act in the same manner as the whole body would act were they present. If the colony continue increasing, it will become necessary to augment the number of the representatives," Thomas Paine, Common Sense, (1776), pps. 6-7.

legislatures[4] and represent the interest of the state in the federal legislature. One contentious issue to be worked out was how many people a representative would have in their district. This was hotly debated and the one of the most important issues in the Constitutional Convention. The issue was the only issue George Washington spoke about.

> "Nathaniel Gorham said that if it was not too late, he would like to suggest that the clause in Article I. giving a representative in Congress to every forty thousand inhabitants, be changed to one in every thirty thousand.
>
> It was a matter upon which the Convention had seriously disagreed; a larger representation would benefit the big states to the disadvantage of the small. Washington stood up to put the question. It must have surprised members when the General, after his summer's silence, suddenly launched into speech. He declared, wrote Madison, 'That although his situation had hitherto restrained him from offering his sentiments on questions depending in the House, and it might be thought, ought now to impose silence on him, yet he could not forbear expressing his wish that the alteration proposed might take place. It was much to be desired that the objections to the plan recommended might be made as few as possible. – **The smallness of the proportion of representatives had been considered by many members of the Convention, an insufficient security for the rights and interests of the people.** He acknowledged that it had always appeared to himself that as among the exceptional parts of the plan; and late as the present moment was for admitting amendments, he thought this of so much consequence that it would give much satisfaction to see it adopted.'
>
> The General's plea, the General's influence were irresistible. Unanimously, the states agreed." (Underlining added.)

---

4   This was later changed by the 17th Amendment which was ratified on April 8, 1913.

Catherine Drinker Bowen, *Miracle At Philadelphia: The Story of the Constitutional Convention May - September 1787* (London: Little, Brown and Company, 1966), p. 257.

This debate between the Federalists and the anti-Federalists continued after the 1787 convention. The Federalists argued that one representative for every 30,000 people was enough.[5] The Anti-Federalists said that was too few to properly represent the citizens.[6] Suffice it to say, this was the biggest issue debated the most by both factions in creating the U.S. Constitution. The Federalist did make the point that there would be a problem if representation did not increase with the population.[7]

2. Where It Is Today

Even though the number that rests in Article I of the Constitution is 30,000 rather than 40,000, the operative language amounts to the mandate that there be no more than one representative for every 30,000 people.[8] Effectively, this means that the districts can be arbitrarily large. Supposedly there was a worry that the citizens would want to have too much representation. Also, there was a belief by the founders that the citizens would be vigilant to constantly demand more representation as time went by and the population grew. That has not been the case. Most citizens do not

5   "... a representative for every thirty thousand inhabitants will render the latter both a safe and competent guardian of the interests which will be confided to it." James Madison, "The Federalist no. 56," *Independent Journal*, 16 Feb. 1788.

6   "... a small representation can never be well informed as to the circumstances of the people, the members of it must be too far removed from the people, in general, to sympathize with them, and too few to communicate with them: a representation must be extremely imperfect where the representatives are not circumstanced to make the proper communications to their constituents, and where the constituents in turn cannot, with tolerable convenience, make known their wants, circumstances, and opinions, to their representatives; where there is but one representative to 30,000, or 40,000 inhabitants, it appears to me, he can only mix, and be acquainted with a few respectable characters among his constituents," "Federal Farmer," Letter VII, (31 Dec. 1787).

7   "The remaining charge against the House of Representatives, which I am to examine, is grounded on a supposition that the number of members will not be augmented from time to time, as the progress of population may demand. It has been admitted, that this objection, if well supported, would have great weight." James Madison, "The Federalist No. 58," *Independent Journal*, 20 Feb. 1788.

8   "Within every successive term of ten years a census of inhabitants is to be repeated. The unequivocal objects of these regulations are, first, to readjust, from time to time, the apportionment of representatives to the number of inhabitants, under the single exception that each State shall have one representative at least; secondly, to augment the number of representatives at the same periods, under the sole limitation that the whole number shall not exceed one for every thirty thousand inhabitants." Madison, "The Federalist No. 58."

know this problem even exists, and slowly, over time, the ratio of citizens to representative has swelled.

For quite some time, the number of representatives did grow since 1790, however, not at the same rate as the population. In fact, the districts kept growing in size until 1912 when the House froze at 435 members. It was the first time that some states actually had a reduction in the number of representatives.

The number of members of the U.S. House of Representatives has been effectively frozen at 435 members since 1912. It did increase to 437 in 1959 when Alaska and Hawaii became states. It was reduced back to 435 after the 1960 Census.

The House was supposed to be the branch of government that was the most in tune with the citizens of the United States and yet, as the population grows, the number of members in the House does not. This has the effect of reducing the value of each citizen's vote and makes the power of each rep that much greater. Today, the average U.S. House district is now over 700,000 people, well above the 40,000 the founders thought was too big!

The districts are certainly too large for the reps to effectively protect our civil rights. The only people who have access to the reps in the House are large donors, union members and corporations. The unfriended individual has no access at all. If they call a Congress member's office, the assistant will answer the phone, but no substantive support will be given.

If the members of the executive or judicial branches of government damage you, the House is not likely going to investigate, so you'd better have enough money to hire a good lawyer. What is worse is that your own tax dollars will be paying the very people who damaged you!

3. Increasing Representation

It is essential to our civil liberties that we increase the size of the U.S. House and in turn, decrease the district size of our federal representatives. It is important for Civil Libertarians to recall that George Washington and the other founders noted that adequate representation was necessary to promote the rights of the citizens. The proposal of one representative for 40,000 was considered to be " . . . an insufficient security for the rights and interests of the people" and 30,000 was advocated.

Simply stated, 435 U.S. House members <u>cannot</u> faithfully represent the 310 million+ people in America. We need more, many more. One recent lawsuit filed in 2010 sought to have the size of the U.S. House increased to either 932 or 1760 members.[9] Mark Meckler, leader of the Tea Party movement has made a call for the House to increase to 4,000 members in speeches. An older lawsuit filed in 1984 called for the U.S. House to increase to over 7,000 members.[10] Under the Constitution, the House could be increased to as many as 10,000 members which, to many, is shocking.

The only thing that has increased in the legislature is the number of assistants. It seems that every year the representatives vote to give themselves more assistants both in their home districts and at the Capital. One credible account placed the the number of assistants between 12,000 and 19,000; that number is simply shocking. Huge corporations and lobbying groups not only kowtow and cater to the reps but also put on lavish parties for these assistants since it oftentimes is they who now write the bills and decide what verbiage to use and how much money to give, instead of those were elected to do so. This is truly scary.

This reform of increasing representation is difficult to achieve. A

---

9   Clemens v. U.S. Dept of Commerce, (Filed 2010, U.S. District Court, Mississippi, Unpublished) No. 10-291, Case No. 3:09-cv-00104
10   Wendelken v. Bureau of the Census, 742 F. 2d 1437 (2d Cir. 1984).

number of lawsuits have unsuccessfully been tried. That is not to say that the courts could not force an increase. It may be the case that the right causes of action have not been tried to date. Perhaps the states need to step in as plaintiffs. Congress could also make the change on its own. However, Congress doing so seems like a long shot, since any addition of more members would necessarily decrease each House member's individual power. [11]

B. The U.S. Senate
1. How It Began
The U.S. Senate was established as part of the Great Compromise after the Constitutional Convention of 1787. The citizens of each state were to be represented by the House and the states would be represented by the U.S. Senate. The U.S. House was apportioned by population and the number of members for each state was based on population. The U.S. Senate had equity in representation so that each state would have 2 members. Initially the Senate members were elected by the state legislatures, but that was changed by the 17th Amendment to the U.S. Constitution (ratified April 8, 1913).

The U.S. Senate began with 26 members and slowly increased as Congress added new states. The Senate had 96 members for almost 40 years until finally, in 1959, Hawaii and Alaska were admitted to the Union, bringing the total number of senators to its current size of 100.

2. Where It Is Today
The U.S. Senate has 100 members. Two are elected at large from each state by the citizens and serve six year terms. Their districts

---

11   "[George] Mason was convinced that once the House began meeting, it would resist efforts to add more members, which he believed necessary for the body to represent the diverse interests of the people. He gave Virginia as an example, where ten members of the House would be elected. He wondered why those individuals would agree to increase the size of the House and thus decrease the relative power that each would exercise. He said they would never 'lessen their own power and influence . . . the greater the number of men among whom any given quantum of power is divided, the less the power of each individual.'" Richard Labunski, James Madison and the Struggle for the Bill of Rights, (New York: Oxford University Press, USA, 2006), p. 83.

do not get reapportioned each census like the U.S. House districts do.

No scholar seems to even suggest a change in the size of the U.S. Senate. One scholar (Professor Terry Smith) recently proposed that U.S. Senate districts be drawn with single member districts much like House seats are drawn. He advances that it would help minorities get elected to such seats. There does not seem to be any clause in the Constitution supporting such a change. However, there is no provision against such a notion.

Professor Smith is correct. If senators were elected by districts rather than at large, there would likely be more senatorial ethnic diversity. However, doing so would put the Senate into the continuous game of gerrymandering. It is interesting to note that U.S. House seats are more electorally stable than Senate seats. This is likely due to the fact that since U.S. senators are elected statewide, their districts are not changed with each census. Since they cannot alter their districts, they are more easily voted out.

3. The Reform
Not only do we need to increase representation in the U.S. House, but we also need to increase the number of U.S. senators. The founders originally proposed that each U.S. senator have a district no larger than 100,000 people. However, in the end they decided to let the U.S. House reflect the population and the states to be represented equally in the U.S. Senate. At the same time, there is too much power in the hands of just these 100 people.

There are two clauses in the U.S. Constitution that mandate each state have the same number of senators for each state.[12] So, any increase that needs to occur will mean that each state would need to have the same number of senators. That is easy enough to maintain.

---

12   Article I sec. 3 and Article V.

A constitutional change that could be made would be to increase the number of members in the U.S. Senate so that each state had three senators. This would make it so that each state would have a senatorial election every two years. Also, the number of senators should be increased in increments of three. At this point each state should minimally have six or more U.S. senators. The expectation by our founders was that as the states would grow in population, there would be a big push to split the state, and thus the number of senators would need to increase, but that has not happened. The last time the Senate increased in size was in 1959 when Hawaii and Alaska were admitted to the Union.

The specific change that needs to be made is a constitutional one and the operative verbiage should openly state that the Senate shall not be fixed in size, but be allowed to increase according to law so long as each state be given equal representation. This would not be an easy reform as it would require an amendment to the U.S. Constitution.

The idea of allowing U.S. senators to be elected by district could merely be legislated and there would likely be many challenges to the constitutionality of such, if that were to occur. The benefits to allowing this would likely outweigh the problems associated with doing that. It would make the districts smaller and more responsive to the citizens. That should always be favored.

II. STATE REPRESENTATION

A. Lower Chambers
1. How It Began
To the founders of the United States, the core of the power of government and the access of the citizens to their government was supposed to be through the state governments and the representation therein. Close representation was a hallmark of the

original founding states. In the 1776 to 1787 the lower chambers of the states had tremendous representation. Some states had a representative in their lower chambers for less than 1,000 people. The state with the largest lower chamber district was Virginia with just one representative for about 4,000 people. Today, only two states, Vermont and New Hampshire, have districts that size.

Yale Law Professor Akhil Reed Amar noted:

> "At the state level, the Revolution had triggered dramatic increases in the size of many a lower house. Several Revolutionary state legislatures dwarfed the new congress in absolute numbers, to say nothing of the ratio of lawmakers to constituents. The Massachusetts House of Representatives alone boasted five times as many members, and the Virginia House of Delegates almost thrice as many, as the House that would represent the entire nation. Only two states, New Jersey and Delaware, had lower houses with fewer than sixty-five members. Overall, some 1,500 assemblymen legislated for the thirteen states respectively, whereas the Philadelphia plan envisioned that less than one-twentieth of that number would legislate for the thirteen states collectively." Akhil Reed Amar, *America's Constitution: A Biography*, (New York: Random House, 2005), p. 77.

2. Where It Is Today

However, for the most part, populations have grown exponentially in the states, but representation has not, though the U.S. founders advocated that it needed to.[13]

Today (2012), the best representation in America is in New

---

13   *"At present some of the States are little more than a society of husbandmen. Few of them have made much progress in those branches of industry which give a variety and complexity to the affairs of a nation. These, however, will in all of them be the fruits of a more advanced population, and will require, on the part of each State, a fuller representation." Madison, "The Federalist No. 56."*

Hampshire with one rep for almost every 3,000 people, which is about the same as it was at the time of the founders. The state with the worst representation is California with one representative for almost a half a million people, which is simply outrageous. The average district size in state lower chambers is about 40,000 persons, which is what was not acceptable to George Washington for the size of a U.S. House district!

The trend has been for states to decrease their own representation over time. Just last year, there was an article telling how states were coping with budget deficits by proposing to decrease representation in their legislatures. However, it has been shown that when legislative representation goes up, government spending goes down.[14] So, removing representatives does not solve the problem.

The most important thing for us to recognize is that representation in the lower chambers is where the common citizen is supposed to have access. We simply do not have access when the districts are this large. When the districts get too big, the representatives' loyalty is no longer to the voter; it begins to flow towards the moneyed interests. These large Assembly districts are too big to give us access to those we elect, or more importantly, to protect our civil liberties.

3. The Reform
The reform is quite simple. A massive increase in the districts of the lower chambers needs to occur. The U.S. founders suggested that the district size of the lower chambers needed to have a 10 to 1 ratio with the districts of the U.S. House. According to our founders, the U.S. House districts were proposed to be about 30,000 to 1. By this authority, that means the lower chambers

---

14   "… larger constituency size was positively related to state government spending. Therefore, smaller legislatures result in larger constituencies, poorer representation, and higher levels of government spending per capita." Mark Thornton and Marc Ulrich, "Constituency Size and Government Spending," Public Finance Review, vol. 27 no. 6, (1999), p. 595.

of each state were supposed to be 3,000 people for each representative. That was indeed where representation began for the founding states. Most states when they joined the Union had this level of representation as well.

In 1850, California had an Assembly member for every 2,500 people. Districts of 3,000 people would give the common citizens direct access to their representatives. A representative would be able to keep the citizens they represent informed. It would also bring the cost of elections way down.

In some states, an increase in representation to that level would amount to a huge legislature. In California, an increase to that level would amount to about 12,000 Assembly members, which is immense. At the same time, there is a need to split many of the larger states in the United States and the only way to do this is to increase representation. If the number of reps does in fact get too large, then the remedy is to invoke Article IV Section 3 of the U.S. Constitution and move to split the state. Our founders noted that liberty existed in small republics much more so than large ones.

A. State Senates
1. How They Began
The thirteen founding colonies, which later became states upon independence, developed their own legislatures, which started as unicameral bodies and later became bicameral as most of us are used to. Political Scientist Pervill Squire did an excellent job of explaining how state senates were formed in the original colonies in his book 101 Chambers:

> "In general, bicameral legislatures emerged from what looked like unicameral bodies in the colonies because of the original distinctions inherent in their colonial systems between councilors as agents of the Crown or proprietors, and representatives as agents of the freemen of the

colonies. The council and the general assembly first became unmistakably separate chambers in Massachusetts. Their process of becoming bicameral was to some extent inchoate. Through the early 1630s, the councilors and the members of the assembly developed different interests and concerns, and these differences led to conflict between them. The most prominent policy dispute between the two groups involved the legal disposition of a case involving a wandering sow. Their disagreement was so great that it led directly to a split. In 1636 a working arrangement was reached between the two groups, the language of which strongly suggests the glimmerings of separate chambers and a bicameral legislature . . . " (Internal citations omitted.) Peverill Squire and Keith E. Hamm, 101 *Chambers: Congress, State Legislatures, and the Future of Legislative Studies (Parliaments and Legislatures Series)*, (Columbus, OH: Ohio State University Press, 2005).

For our founders, bicameral legislatures were considered to be a key trait of Republican government.[15] In the beginning Vermont, Pennsylvania and Georgia had unicameral legislatures. Quickly, they followed the direction of all states and became bicameral. Today, only Nebraska has a unicameral legislature.

The form of a state senate varied differently in each state, however, they were generally anchored in local governments, that is until the decisions of Baker v. Carr, 369 U.S. 186 (1962) and then Reynolds v. Sims, 377 U.S. 533 (1964). Both of these cases mandate equal sized districts (in population) for each chamber. There was a clause in both cases that allowed some deviation for political subdivisions.[16] Ironically, no state had a provision that

---

15   "Even for other, more tangible, elements in the republican ideal, such as structural arrangements, the impact of the clause is problematical. Bicameralism, for example, was central to republicanism of the founders." William M. Wiecek, The Guarantee Clause of The U.S. Constitution, (Ithaca, NY: Cornell University Press, 1972), p. 27.

16   This was directly clarified in the case of Brown v. Thompson, 462 U.S. 835 (1983): "Some deviations from

gave equal representation to their political subdivisions.

For instance, California had (and still has) 40 senators and 58 counties. So, California could not apply the one-county one-senator theory. So, the senators from each state were divorced from the municipalities they had represented before. If California did have 58 or 116 senators, it could have parity in the Senate among counties even if there is a huge deviation in population.

2. Where It Is Today
Today, all the state senates are divorced from their local governments. In fact, there is little difference between state assemblies and their senate counterparts other than the size of their districts. There should be a connection between the state senates and local government in the states. In California, most counties have to hire lobbyists to advance their interests in Sacramento in both chambers.

When we look at the district sizes for state senates, we see the smallest is North Dakota with one state senator for every 14,000 people. Wyoming is not far back with one senator for about every 19,000 people. Those are decent sizes. However, on the other side of the spectrum, California and Texas have outrageously large Senate districts. Texas senators have districts of over 800,000 people. California's Senate districts are approaching one million people which is simply outrageous. The Senate districts of Texas and California are larger than the current U.S. House districts at more than 700,000 people.

3. The Reform
The needed reform is to increase the number of state senate reps

---

population equality may be necessary to permit the States to pursue other legitimate objectives such as 'maintain[ing] the integrity of various political subdivisions' and 'provid[ing] for compact districts of contiguous territory.' But an apportionment plan with population disparities larger than 10% creates a prima facie case of discrimination, and therefore must be justified by the State, the ultimate inquiry being whether the plan may reasonably be said to advance a rational state policy and, if so whether the population disparities resulting from the plan exceed constitutional limits."

in the states where their districts are large (which is most of them). No state senate district should be more than 20,000 people.

Also, each county of a state should have at least one representative in the Senate for each county as is allowed according to the precedents of the U.S. Supreme Court since it advances a legitimate state interest. The lower chamber reps should be tied to the constituents and their civil liberties, whereas the state senators should have their interest tied to local commerce of the state.

III. LOCAL REPRESENTATION

A. County Government
1. How It Began
It is not clear to me when county government was first established in the western sense. Charlemagne established his empire and ruled Europe through its counties. Apparently, under his regime, each county had a lord, a member of the clergy and a supreme judicial court of seven judges.

In England, each county had a count[17] and a shire reeve (a sheriff). The counts often acquired their land initially through conquest and then kept it through hereditary lineage. The sheriffs were for some time appointed by the crown and then later elected by either the count or the people. One authority suggests that the size and shape of a county was supposed to represent the distance the sheriff could ride a horse in a single day.

County government was brought to America and emulated here. As counties were developed, so were county governments established, but often, in rural areas, the only county government was the grand jury. However, most counties chose elective representatives. Just as with other levels of government, county

---

17 Apparently "Counts preferred to be called "Earls" though both terms are reciprocal.

representation has not increased with the population.

County government typically provides state services to citizens of that state living in that county. These services include health and welfare and other social services. This is particularly true in the more rural counties that do not have cities in them. Many rural citizens only have access to county government. The U.S. Census is collected on a county by county basis. Grand juries are generally picked by each county in the states where that institution still exists. County government is also where district attorneys tend to be elected from, as are sheriffs and other executives such as election officials. Many counties still elect county coroners as well.

2. Where It Is Today
There is a wide spectrum of representation today in county government. Some time ago, Connecticut did away with their county government and transferred the services that are generally provided to the state or city government. It seems to have been a very successful move as it cut costs in that small state.

The average representation across the states in the counties is 12 county commissioners per county. However, the representation in the counties as far as district size varies greatly. The extremes are quite great. In California, Alpine is the smallest county and has just under 1,200 people. Alpine has five supervisors, so each supervisor has about 240 people to represent. That is more than adequate. On the other end of the spectrum is Los Angeles County. Its population is almost ten million people. So, each of their five supervisors has almost two million people to represent, which is outrageous. Most states do not have a population as large as these supervisorial districts.

Another issue of interest is the fact that there are numerous county boards. These include community college boards, county health boards, airport boards, utility boards and so forth. These positions tend to be elected at large or by district with only their entity's boundaries taken into account. These boards are often hidden from public purview and most citizens are not aware of them or their jurisdictional powers. Money often flows to these boards from the federal and state government with conditions that often usurp the interest of the citizens.

3. The Reform

First, there needs to be more reps in the counties for the citizens. Looking back at Los Angeles, we see a prime example where each of their supervisors has two million constituents. A need for an increase there should be obvious. Other California Counties, such as Orange and San Diego, which have one supervisor for every 600,000 people, should have more as well. This then invites the question: how many people should a supervisor represent? This is a difficult question to answer. It is likely the case that county representation should be closer than state level representation.

Second, these county level boards need to be consolidated centrally and made into subcommittees of the county boards of supervisors (or county commissioners as the case may be).

Third, some of these enormous counties need to be split into smaller counties. It is simple as that. However, to do this would require an increase in state government representation. This means we would need more state senators and Assembly members. They in turn would then be able to sit down and pass laws to increase representation at the county level and draw new county lines within the large counties. Many states have not drawn new county lines in over a century.

B. City Government
1. How They Began

Cities have been with us for centuries. Throughout history, nations tended to be governed by their rulers in their capital cities. In

England, cities seemed to have originated with Alfred the Great as a means of defense for the nation. These centers of defense quickly grew into centers of commerce and industry, which they still are today.

Though cities were not originally built in America with the primary goal of defense, cities were population centers and commerce flourished in them. In early America, local government was very close to the citizens. These sparsely populated cities had numerous representatives. Many of them followed European cities and were bicameral.

2. Where It Is Today

Cities, much like counties, are all over the map when it comes to representation. There are small cities with excellent representation and there are large cities with sparse representation. The latter is the trend. Just as at other levels of government, the population grows and the number of representatives does not. This tends to go on unnoticed for decades as the population expands.

Another trend that has occurred with great proliferation in cities is the election of representatives at large rather than by district. What this means is that all of the representatives of a city are voted upon by the entire city, rather than each corner of a city electing their own representative for a smaller district. City mayors are quite traditionally elected at large, but council members can be elected either by district or at large. Small and moderate cities now tend to have at large districts.

At-large districts were used by many southern cities to keep Blacks from getting elected to office. Consider, for example, a small city of 20,000 people, with 60% White voters and 40% Black and four city council members and one mayor. If the council members were elected by district, then the Blacks could elect one and maybe two representatives based on population. However, when elections are done at large, Blacks tend to be kept from getting elected at all. The same thing happens in a city that is 60% Republican and 40% Democrat. If there are districts, then at least one Democrat could get elected. However, at large, the only way that a Democrat would get elected is if there was a large cross over vote. We find that people tend to vote with their party.

Just as in counties, the proliferation of boards of directors also occurs in city government. This includes school boards, library boards, sewer and water boards. These boards may be elected either at large or by district. However, the members of these boards are all over the place and the common citizen cannot keep track of their actions. So further, these boards also often have the power of taxation and eminent domain. This means that upon simple majority, they can often raise property taxes or issue bonds. This also means that they can take property. These boards generally have a small membership of five or seven and a majority can usually carry the vote. So, on a five member board, three can raise taxes. Or a seven member board, four can carry a motion.

Each of these numerous boards can propose bond issues. Let us consider in a hypothetical city that there may be a fire district, a school board, a sewer district and an airport board. When each goes for money, they generally consider their own needs above all others and they tend to ask for as much as they can. The ideal allocation of resources may be towards one interest rather than the others. However, these boards tend not to consider the interests or the needs of the city above their own board's interest.

What often happens is that each board passes a bond to ask the citizens to vote for their bond, which is generally for as much money as they can get regardless of city (and citizens') needs. Sometimes projects that are not a high priority pass, and then projects that are of higher priority do not pass because the citizens just passed a bond, raised their taxes and now the citizens no longer want to foot the bill for a new project even if the community needs it.

However, if we consolidated all of these boards together and made their jurisdiction a committee to the city council, something different would happen. Amounts would be voted upon for projects out of each committee. Then, the projects would have to go to the city as a whole. The capacity of the city to borrow would be much less than the proposed projects. Then, the representatives of the city would need to decide which projects are really needed, and a mixed basket of goods based upon the collective needs of the citizens would occur, rather than one big project for whoever could get it passed first. This is the better model.

Another concern with these boards is the fact that they get grants from various state and federal agencies. Often the mandates of these agencies are contrary to the will of the electorate. However, the boards are likely to vote for them because of the extra incentive cash that is added to them. This is often cash that is needed to help pay down unfunded, employee, retirement funds. So, in this light, consolidating these boards would amount to giving the citizens more of their sovereignty back.

That is important because city government is generally the level of government that most people have direct access to. City governments are where most of the representation should be.

3. The Reform
The first reform is to simply mandate that all cities have single member districts for their councils so that the citizens have access to a representative.

Second, the legislative terms of the representatives in cities need to be cut down to one or two years so that those in office cannot easily ignore the people they represent. We see a proliferation of city council terms of four years, which is simply too long.

Third, there needs to be more reps in most city councils. The number should not be static for the entire city, but based on district size. Ideally, each city rep should be no more than 300 people or so. Perhaps more for larger cities, but I am speaking of ideal circumstances.

Last, the city boards should be consolidated and turned into an upper chamber for cities. Then they need to be given single member districts and perhaps a legislative term of two to three years. All their prior duties such as library board and so forth should be turned into a committee of the chamber. Perhaps the boards could be turned into the second chamber for cities.

IV. REPRESENTATION

A. The Main Duties of a Representative Body
Regardless of the many tasks that representative body many engage in, a Representative body has two duties in chief and these have been anciently held:

1. Take Petitions for Redress of Grievances
"The people shall not be restrained from peaceably assembling and consulting for their common good; nor from applying to the Legislature by petitions, or remonstrances, for redress of their grievances." James Madison, The Introduction of the Bill of Right in Congress, The Annals of Congress, House of Representatives, First Congress, 1st Session, pp 448-460.

2. To Investigate and Inform
"It is the proper duty of a representative body to look diligently into every affair of government and to talk much about what it sees. It is meant to be the eyes and the voice, and to embody the wisdom and will of its constituents. Unless Congress have and use every means of acquainting itself with the acts and the disposition of the administrative agents of the government, the country must

be helpless to learn how it is being served; and unless Congress both scrutinize these things and sift them by every form of discussion, the country must remain in embarrassing, crippling ignorance of the very affairs which it is most important that it should understand and direct. The informing function of Congress should be preferred even to its legislative function." (Cited by the U.S. Supreme Court in US v. Rumely in 1953).

All other functions that most of us associate with a representative body, be they lawmaking (in truth a part of the petitioning process) or budgeting and taxation, these are the most important and essential to our liberties. However, in order to properly execute these functions, there needs to be enough members of a legislative body to take petitions and investigate. So, I ask openly:

How can 80 Assembly members and 40 senators in California take petitions from the near 40 million people they represent? They can't! So, what happens is, the petitions that do get answered are the ones that come with either large checks attached to them or from people who give regularly. Anyone who is damaged by the current system needs to be in the next category, which is to be able to afford a lawyer to advance their interests in a trial court since they have been priced out of the legislature.

How can 435 House members and 100 U.S. senators investigate the thousands of federal agencies we now have? They simply cannot. So, we should not be surprised when the SEC is not able to uncover a scandal such as the one Bernie Madoff perpetrated for decades since Congress is not overseeing the SEC or any other agency in a substantive manner. In fact, we should expect all such agencies to act poorly and in fact to waste the resources we send them (through taxation) and, in some cases, hurt the very people who finance their operations. (That would be us!)

How can five supervisors oversee the government agencies in Los

Angeles County and the 10 million people who live there? They cannot possibly do it. The supervisors begin taking on hordes of assistants and those assistants (who are unelected) become autonomous. The agencies themselves become autonomous as well since it is the taxes from the citizens which are now used to finance the elections of the supervisors. So, one hand washes another and the citizens are left holding the tax bill.

B. The Benefits to This Reform Would Be

There are numerous benefits to increasing representation, too numerous to place here. However, these benefits can be put into key categories that are simple for those who are reform-minded to understand.

1. Better Access

An increase in representation would give the common citizens greater access to their representatives. This means direct access to the representatives themselves and not the assistants. The modern trend has been for the representatives to increase the number of assistants rather than their own enumeration. A voter should have access to the person they vote for, not to whom they delegate you.

When districts such as the senate districts in California reach one million people, that is the number of people who also have (or should have) access to the representative. When the district gets this large, the factor that determines your access is money or prestige. The only other way to get access is some other form of notoriety such as a surge in the media, but all of us should have access to the representative based on the matters that we need to see them about.

2. Competitive Elections and Greater Participation

The larger the district gets, the more it costs to run. If the district is big or gets bigger, it becomes more difficult to contact the people in that district. So, print media, mass mailers and signs become more important. The voters are more detached from the electoral process. Fewer questions are asked. Issues of some importance are swept to the side.

If a voter lives in a district such as New Hampshire's or Vermont's lower chamber, there are only between 3,000 and 4,000 people. A large percentage of those people do not vote. Races come down to between 1,000 and 2,000 people voting. An incumbent or a person challenging the incumbent can visit their whole district and perhaps more than once. Those candidates can learn what the needs and concerns of the people are in that districts. If the voters reject a candidate, the candidate often knows why. So, each voter feels that they have been heard and the winner can consider himself well instructed by the voters of their district on what to do in the legislature. If a representative in a small district is not attentive to the needs of the citizens, they could more easily replace them with someone who is attentive.

The opposite is true for large districts. When a district is large, like the Texas Senate districts which are over 800,000 in size, voters have little to no contact with their representative. The senators are less informed as to the goings on in the district, and they need to have lots of money to communicate with those in their district. Incumbents fare better since they can use their office and committee positions to garner the money they need for elections. Their electoral challengers generally do not enjoy this advantage, and this is why these challengers usually lose. In fact re-election rates are over 90% and this is the very reason why. It is also why reforms are frequently stymied.

The current formula to beating incumbents in large districts is either to find a local millionaire to run against them or to wait until the census each decade when the districts are redrawn and the current representative decides that their negatives are too high to try to meet the new voters! It is also much more difficult to gerrymander small districts.

It is also much more difficult to tamper with elections in small electoral districts. In large districts, it is almost impossible to see if ballots had been stuffed or even tell who voted and who did not. If a district is small, any person can go through the rolls and see if voters are real or still alive or even live in the district, so they may be properly purged. The larger the district, the more difficult this task becomes.

3. Diversity
I shall divide this into three categories: Partisan, Ethnic/Gender and Economic.

Partisan: Members of third parties, such as Libertarians, would also fare better electorally with smaller districts. In fact, if representation was expanded at all levels, the Libertarian party would be an electoral force to be reckoned with. Money would not be as important to the electoral process. More third party members are elected from small districts than large ones. New Hampshire has had several Libertarians elected over the years and after this next redistricting if the state's lower chamber will be forced into single member districts, many Libertarians will be elected.

Vermont not only has six Green Party members, but they also have a U.S. senator who is a third party member as well. Smaller districts bode well for members of third parties. Also, when districts are large, those voting tend to go down their ballot and choose according to party and search only for Ds or Rs. When districts are small, the political label is not as important. People tend to know the people they are voting for personally.

Ethnic/Gender: When representation increases, the ethnic diversity in the makeup of a legislature goes up. It starts to reflect the cross section of the community it represents. When representation goes up, more people of color and more women get elected to the legislature.

Economic: An increase in representation would also amount to a greater economic diversity. There would be more people from each economic class and vocational background. The rich always have access to government. Freedom for all requires that the poor have some part as well.

As it has been shown above, the smaller the electoral district gets, the less it costs to run for office, this in turn gives a greater economic cross section which means the legislative body would have a greater experiential background, which itself is a boon for legislating. It amounts to a system of inclusiveness, not the oligarchy we have inherited which more and more seems to aggrandize itself in all ways possible.

4. Accountability
With an increase in representation would come more persons capable of holding the members of the executive and judicial departments accountable. The 435 U.S. House members and 100 U.S. senators cannot watch the over 1,000 federal judges and the hundreds of federal agencies and the thousands of federal employees in those departments. More representatives would allow that to happen. Also, as noted above, if they did not respond to these needs, we would be more capable of voting them out and voting in someone who was able to take care of our problems.

We need to pick only one of the many scandals in DC to see that Congress is not capable of overseeing the other branches of government, even though oversight as their check and balance on the other branches is one of the most important duties of the legislature.

5. Fiscal Restraint

A study provided by the Mises Institute shows that as representation goes up, government spending drops.[18] The simple rationale is that as the number of representatives goes up, consensus for spending bills goes down. It becomes more difficult to pass spending bills and more difficult to find an unrepresented class of people upon which to foist the cost while the benefit is handed to someone else. So, proper taxation improves, where the person who benefits from the spending will also bear the cost.

The effect of this will be a decrease in the number of government agencies and the monopolies they enjoy. This means more services would be provided by the free market. Cost considerations will be put back into actions, and production would end up going to those most capable of producing, and not to those who have the best political connections, and are most able to gouge the rest of us for their ever-increasing costs, retirements and other forms of feather bedding. So, adding representation will have the effect of greater fiscal restraint, less wasteful spending and, eventually, lower taxes for all of us.

6. Better Problem Solving

With more representatives, more time would be taken to properly solve problems. With competitive elections, a cross section of representation and better access, the problems we have, be they political, environmental, social or otherwise, would be handled more fairly and more justly. Many of our founders have noted that justice is the end of civil government.

7. Enhanced Civil Liberties

The final aspect of all the above advantages to this reform is that our civil liberties would be promoted. More representation would give us the civil rights we want to enjoy. It is the reason we form

---

18   Mark Thornton and Marc Ulrich, "Constituency Size and Government Spending," *Public Finance Review*, vol. 27 no. 6, (Nov. 1999), pps. 588-598.

a government, and if government does not achieve this, then we should pull ourselves from it. Of all the reforms that I can propose to make the system better, this is simply the most important. The benefits to increasing representation are numerous because access to your representative is the key to all rights in a representative government. The Federalist even went so far as to say that having a large representative body that involves as many factions as possible to represent the great cross section of America was necessary for civil rights.[19]

V. CONCLUSION

Of the three branches of government, the legislature is the most important to the citizens and their liberties. Since the founding of America, it has been the most neglected and overlooked. To at least one of the anti-Federalists, representation was the most important aspect of forming good government.[20]

To many, this so called reform may sound counter-intuitive. It often seems like "increasing government" (which Libertarians are very much against), but it is not. Government is really all the persons in a polity, from those holding the reigns of power to those paying for it. The question comes down to: who has access to the legislature and who does not? By increasing representation, we increase that access to all persons and make it more accountable and responsive to all. We also make the other branches of government accountable as well.

Few things are as powerful or as important as a stable government.

---

19   "In a free government the security for civil rights must be the same as that for religious rights. It consists in the one case in the multiplicity of interests, and in the other in the multiplicity of sects. The degree of security in both cases will depend on the number of interests and sects; and this may be presumed to depend on the extent of country and number of people comprehended under the same government." James Madison, "The Federalist no. 51," Independent Journal, 6 Feb. 1788.
20   "I am in a field where doctors disagree; and as to genuine representation, though no feature in government can be more important, perhaps, no one has been less understood, and no one that has received so imperfect a consideration by political writers." (Underlining added.) "The Founders' Constitution, 13, Representation," Federal Farmer VII, 31 Dec. 1787, Chap. 13, Doc. 22.

We should all be working toward it. The best, most certain way to achieve this is to increase representation in the legislatures at every level of government from national to local.

"Structuralism"

The Constitution is in effect the contract and set of rules that the governors are supposed to follow for the rights that the rest of us are supposed to enjoy. However, the proper structure in that government is essential to preserving that proper balance between government and governed.

There are many legal scholars who profess varying views on matters of law. Some are Constitutionalists, others are Originalists sometimes known as Textualists, who believe in the original writings of the Constitution. Others are so-called Liberal Lions of the more progressive camp where they are most concerned with civil liberties. Others still are legal realists who believe in strict federalism and in states' rights and non-interference by the federal government.

I am an advocate of "Structuralism," since it is the structure of government that underlies all the systems that the various legal minds espouse. The structure of a government is essential to maintaining our rights. If the structure of government is not formed properly or not maintained, then neither shall be our rights.

Libertarians well know Ayn Rand warned that "Potentially, a government is the most dangerous threat to man's rights: it holds a legal monopoly on the use of physical force against legally disarmed victims." The best way to break this monopoly and ensure against this force is to make all citizens involved in as much of the governmental process as possible.

The key place to do this is in the legislature, and the method is to promote participation in it, so that the many do not become mere subjects controlled by the few.

Michael Warnken, President, Project Commonwealth
projectcommonwealth.com

www.ingramcontent.com/pod-product-compliance
Lightning Source LLC
Chambersburg PA
CBHW050130280326
41933CB00010B/1313